MYSTERIOUS MASKS

&

BEAUTIFUL FEMALE FACES

COLORING BOOK

2 BOOK BUNDLE

Mysterious MASKS Coloring Book

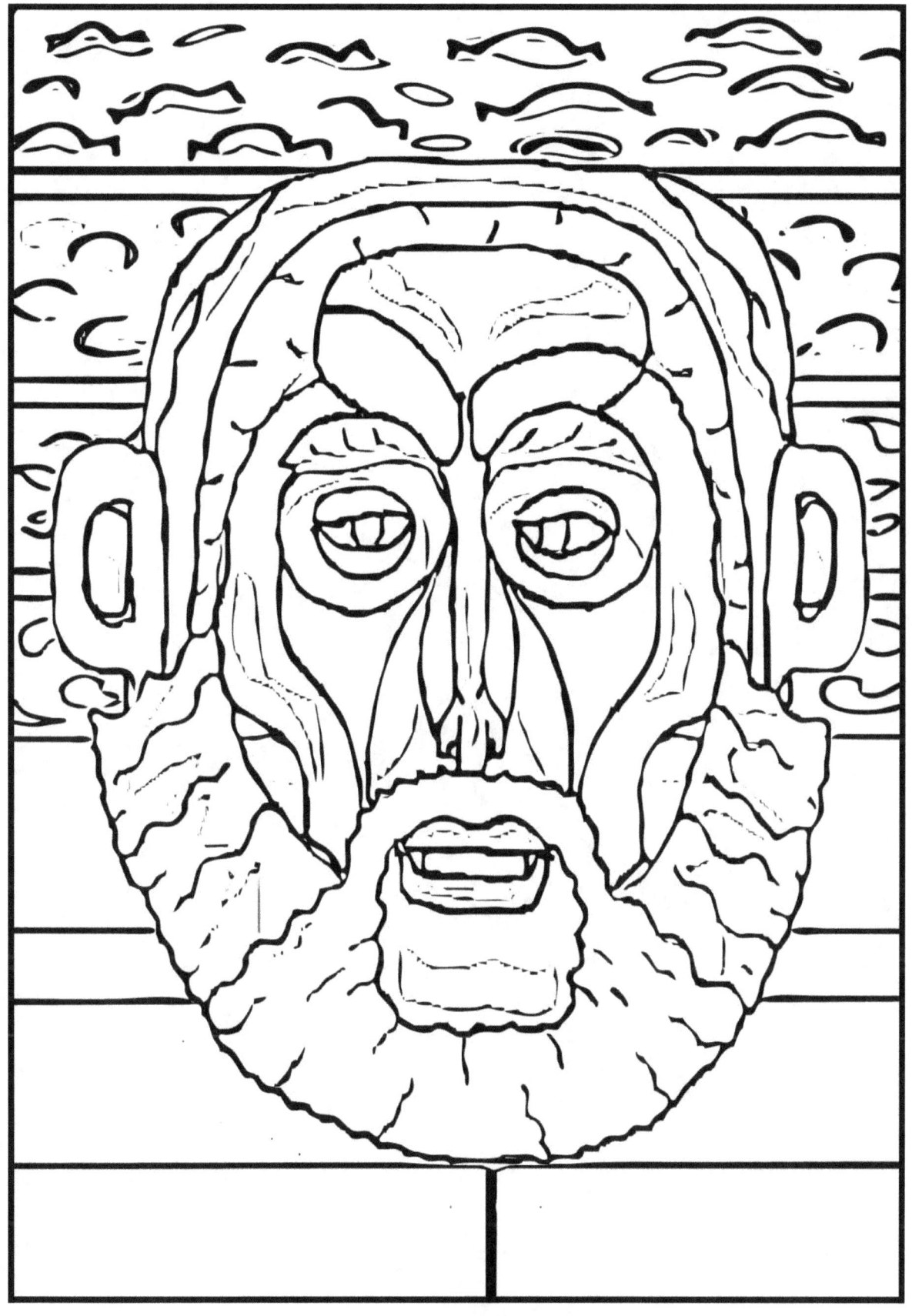

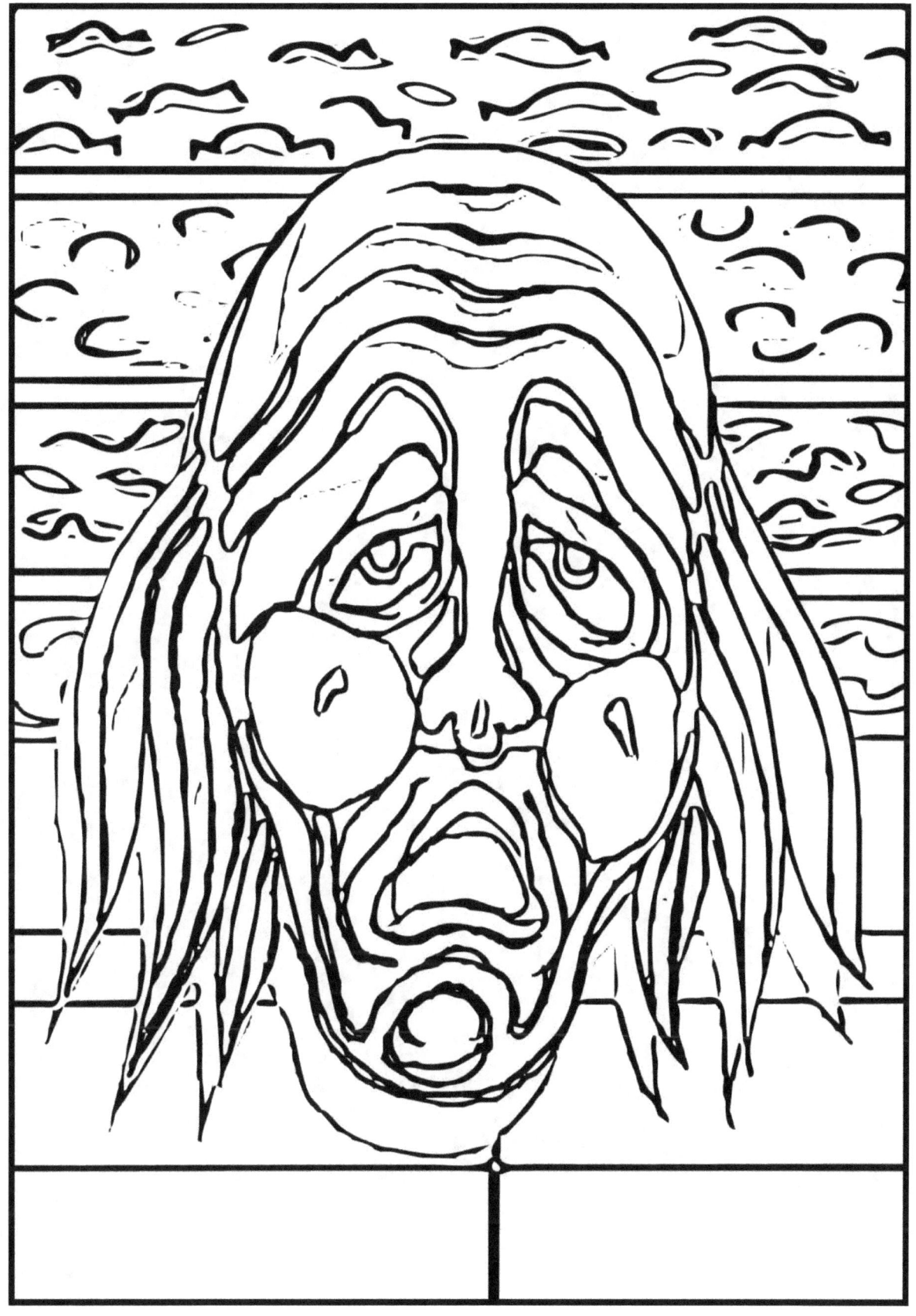

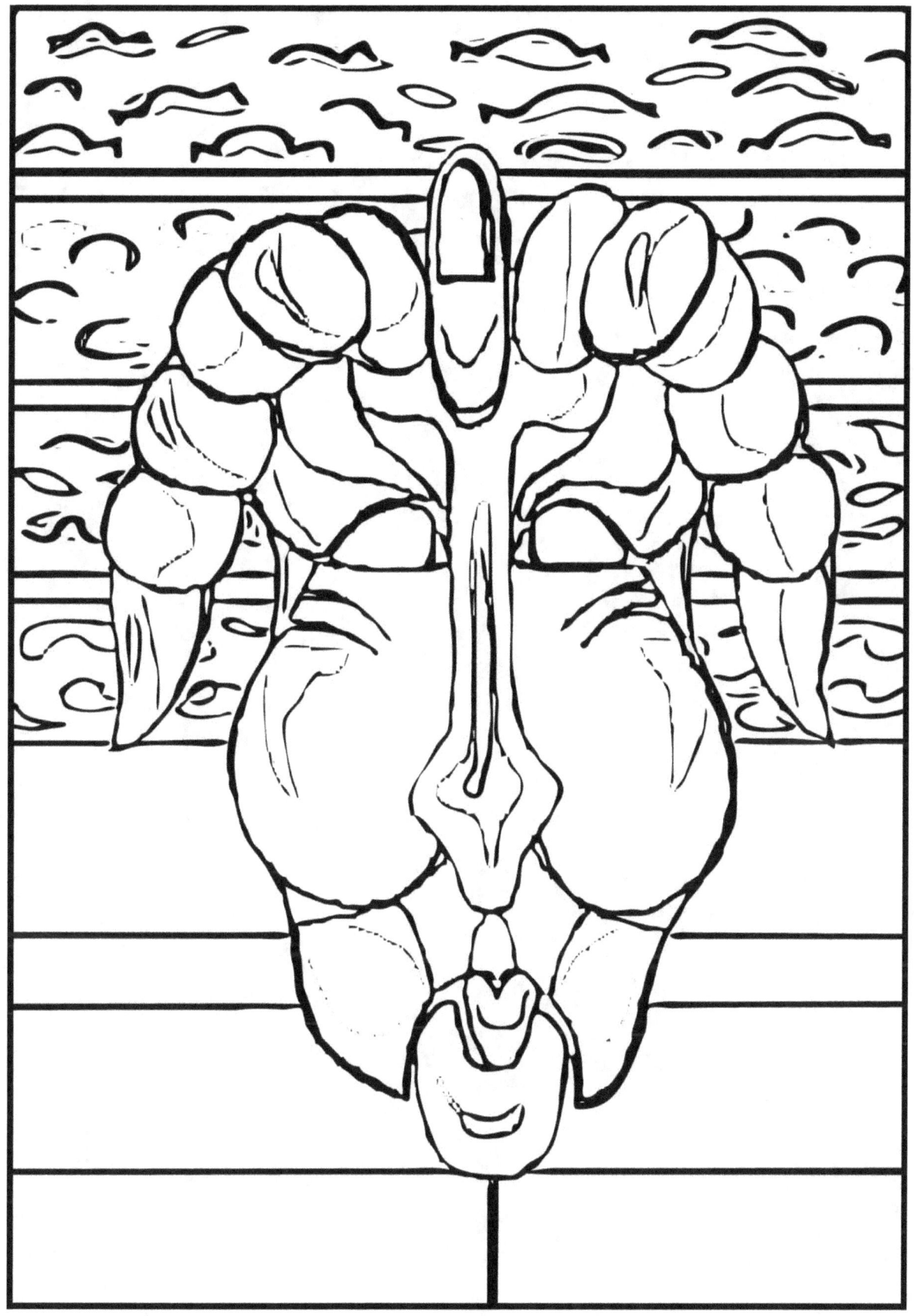

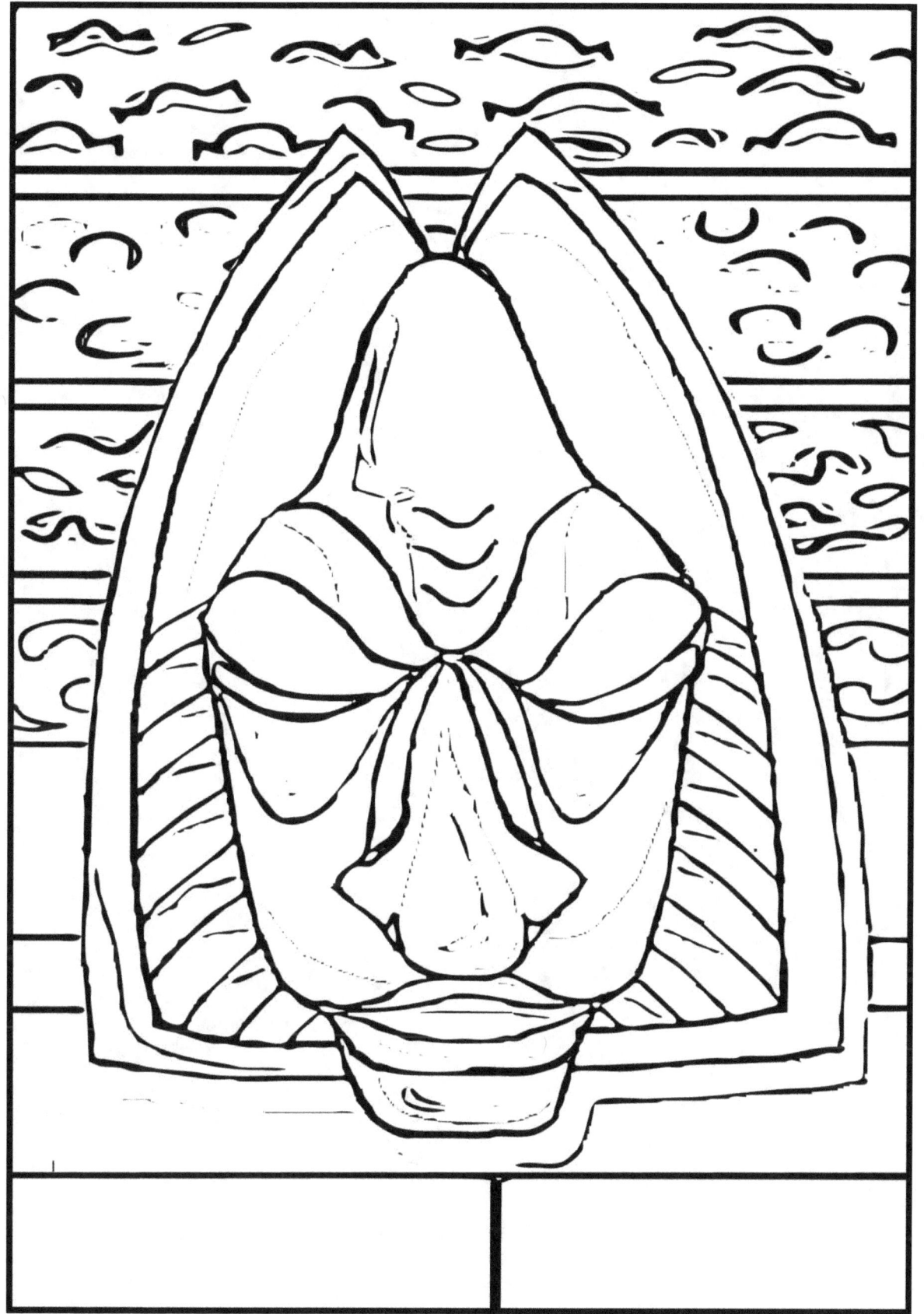

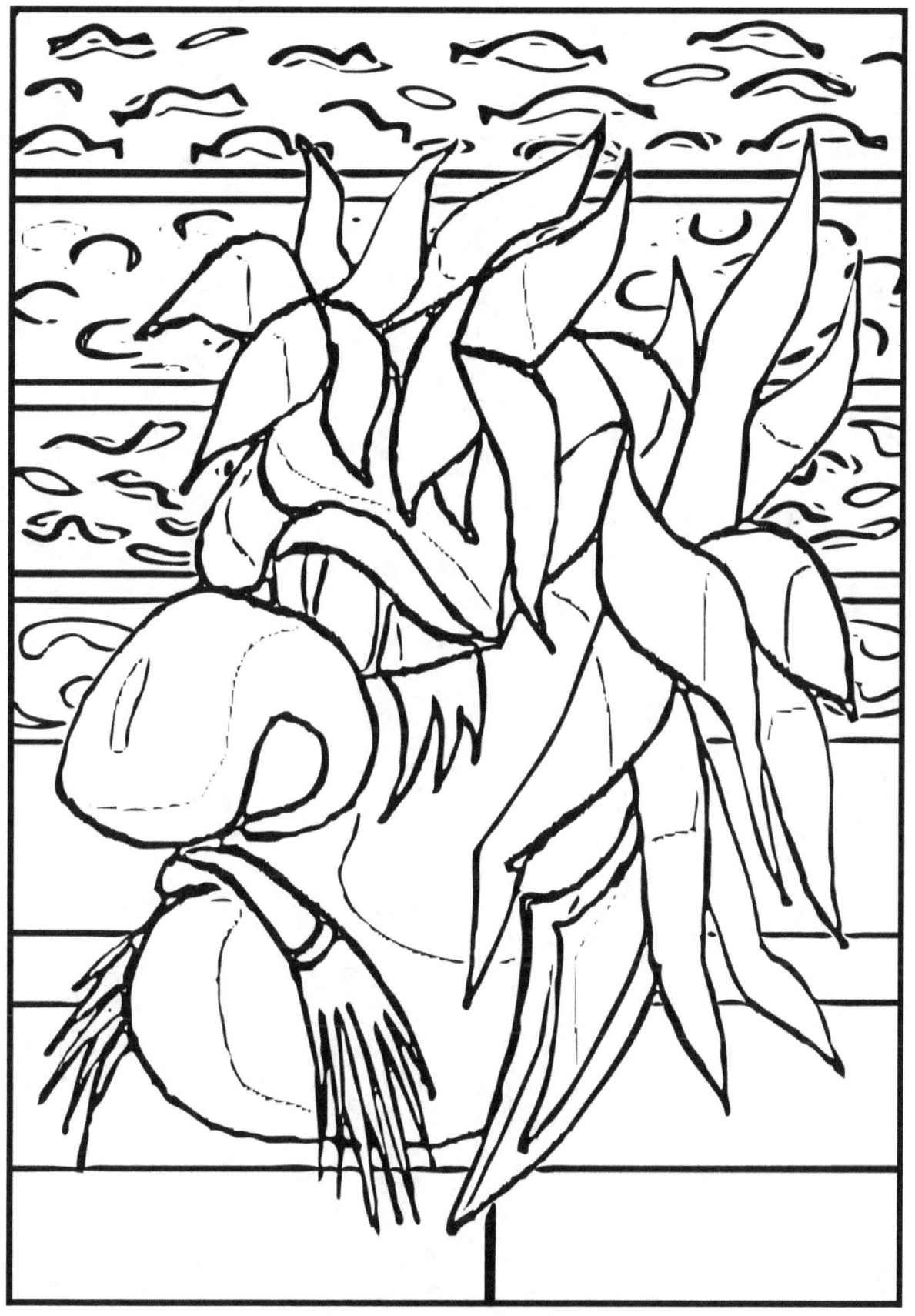

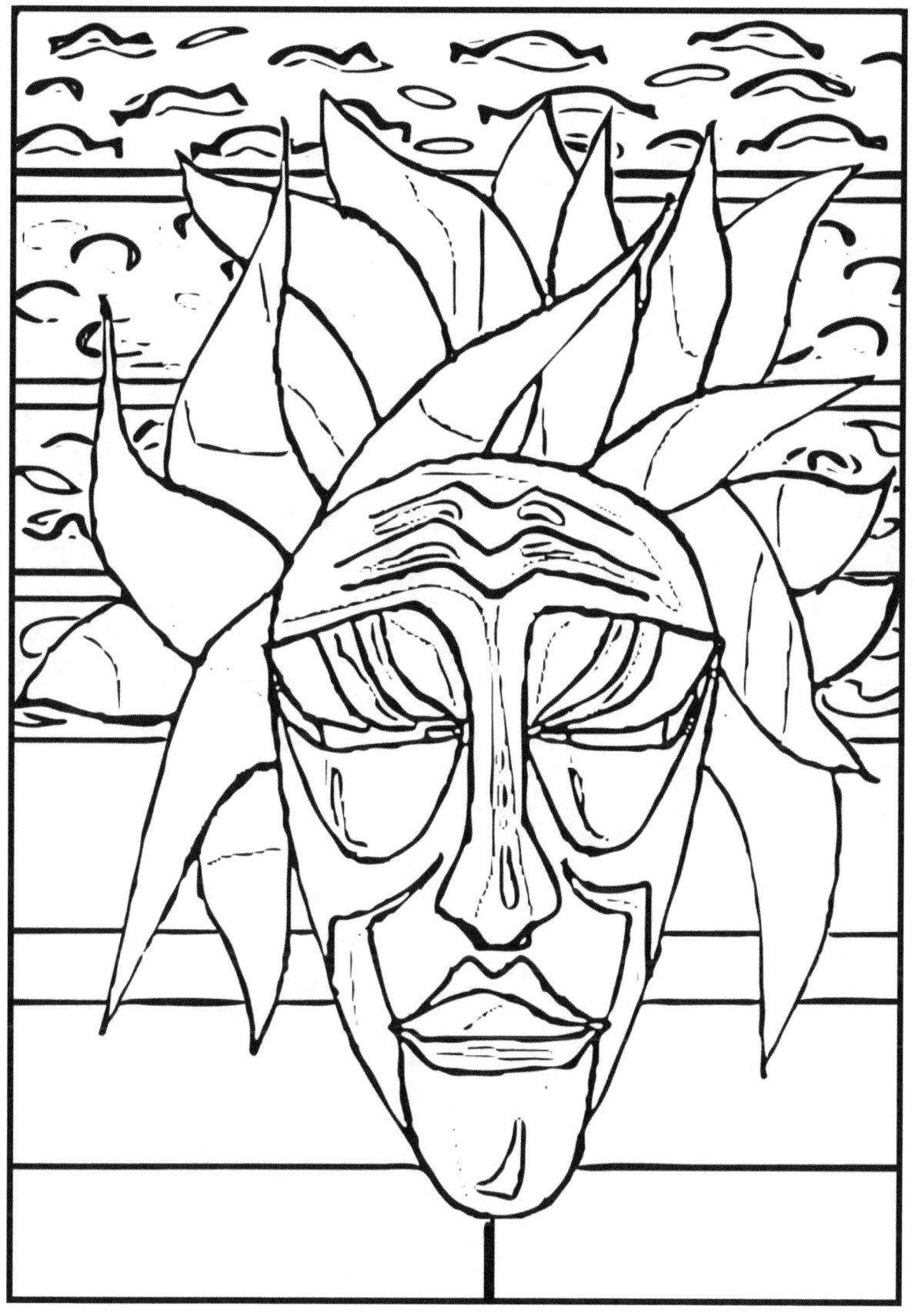

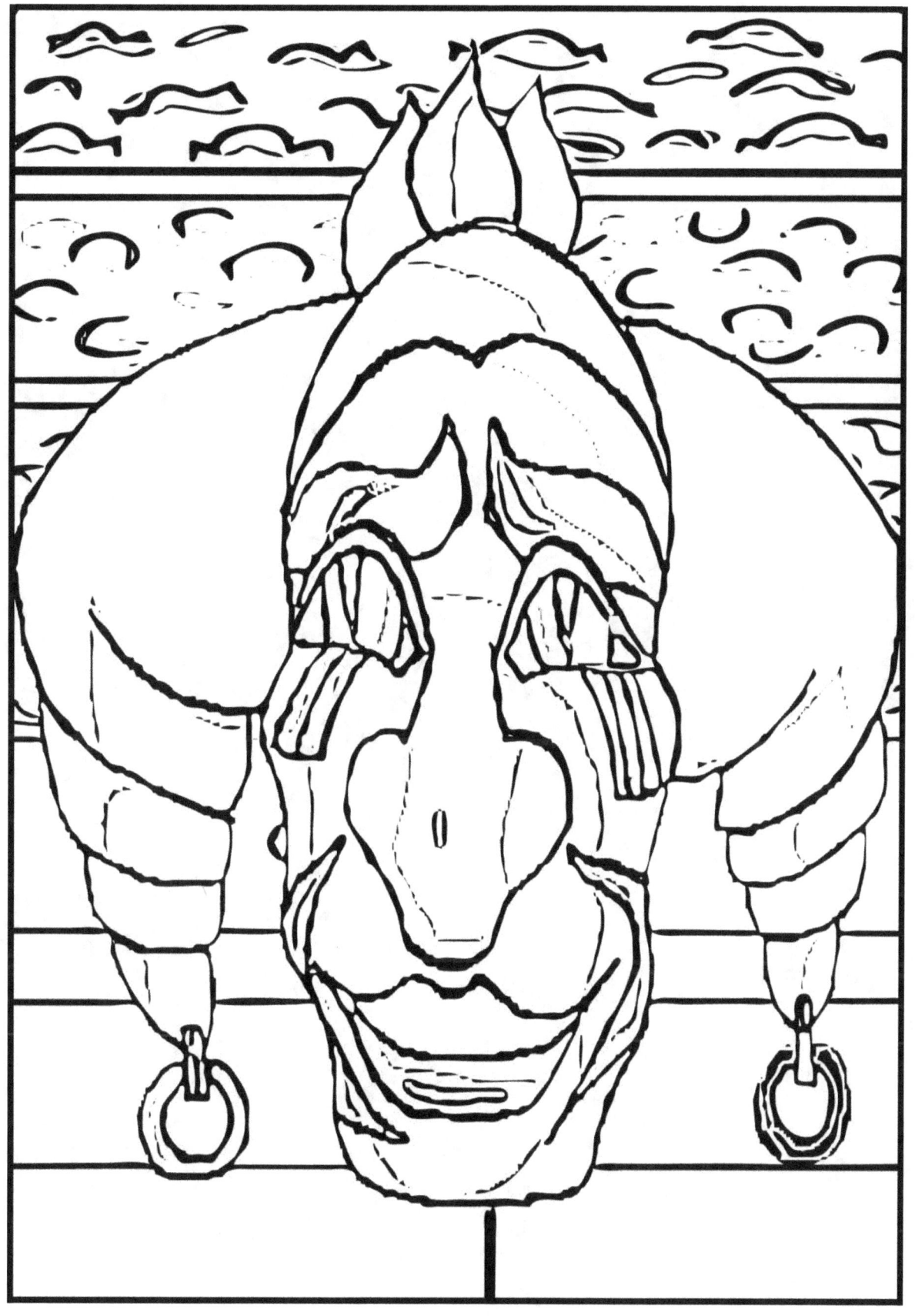

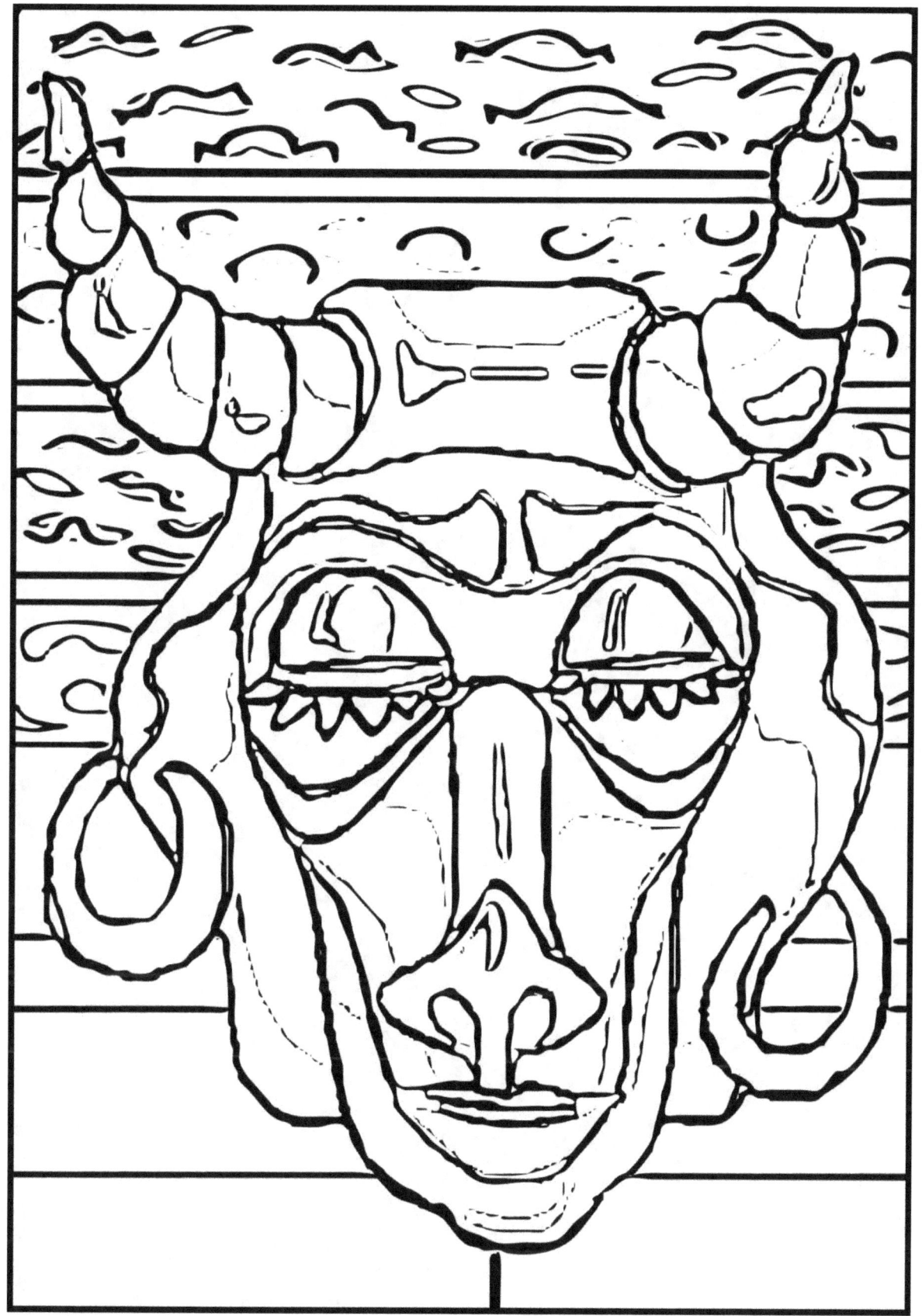

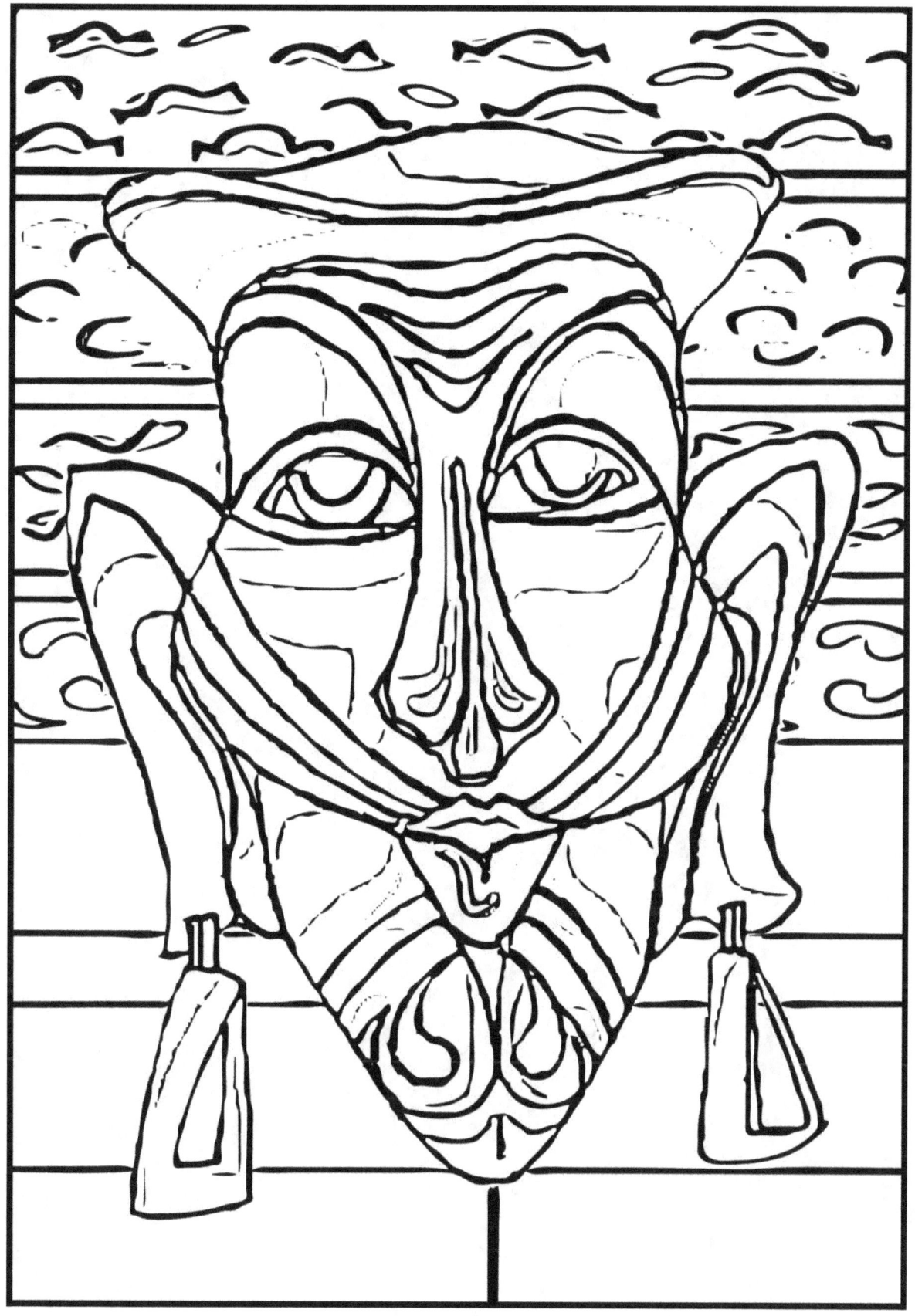

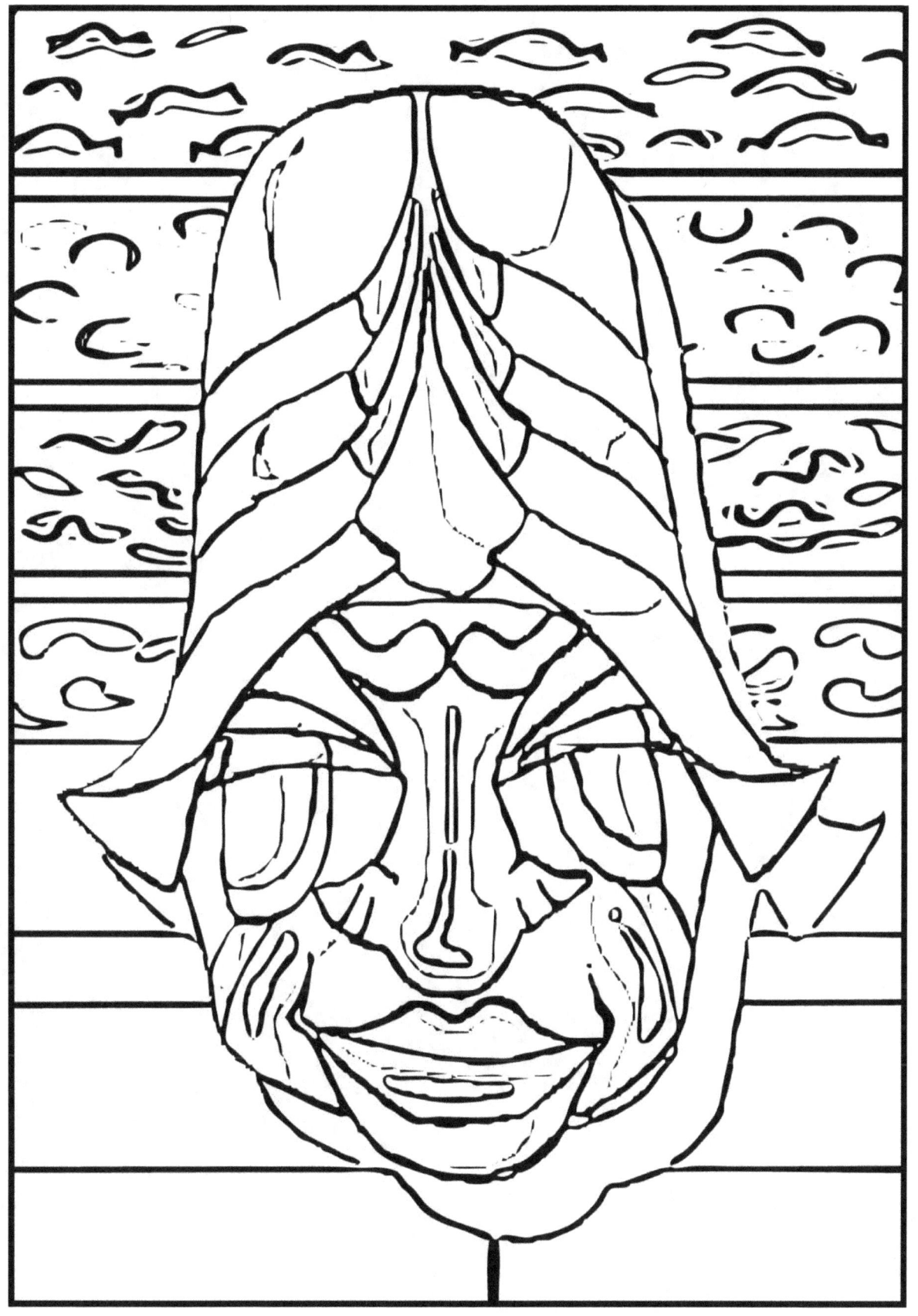

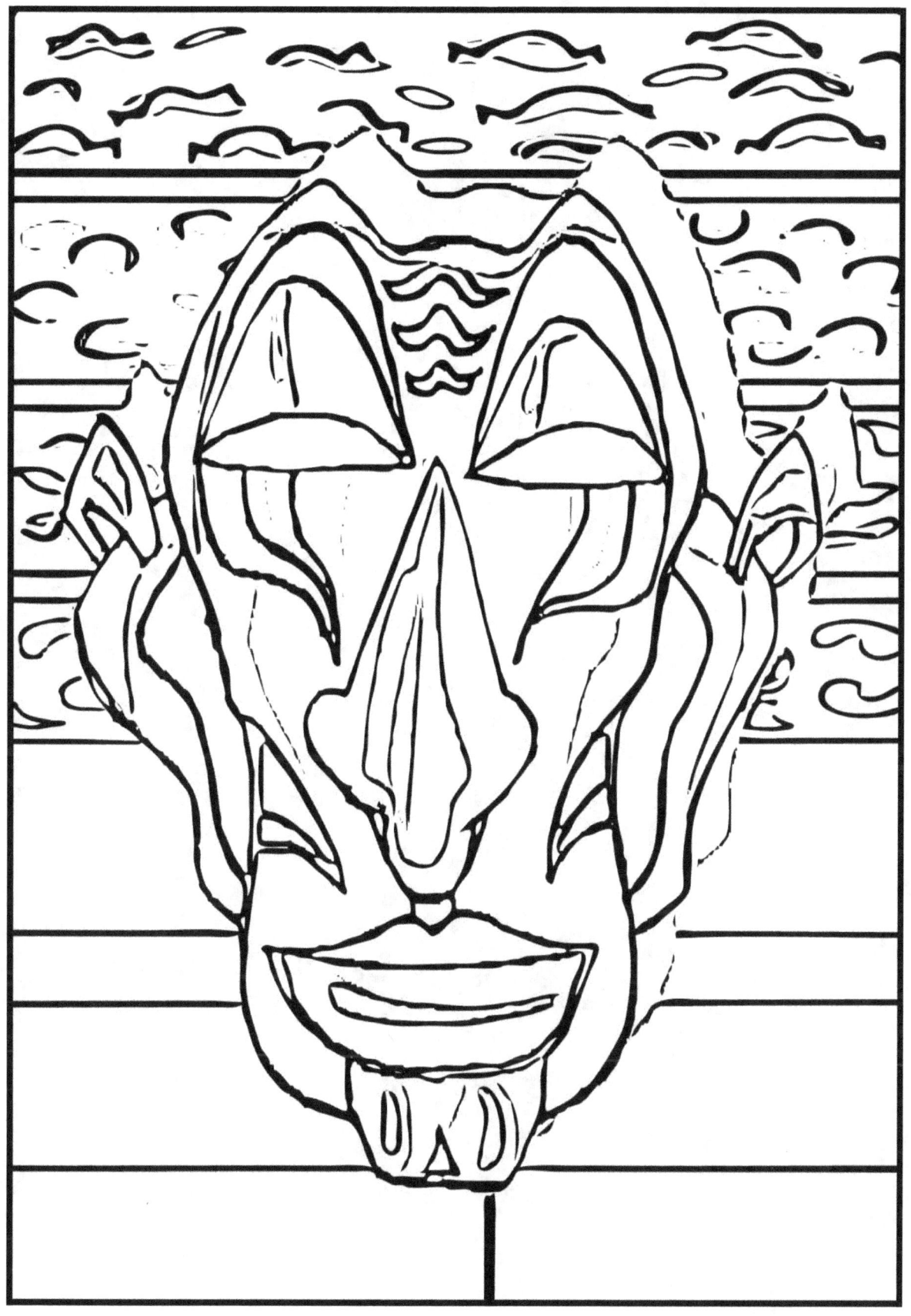

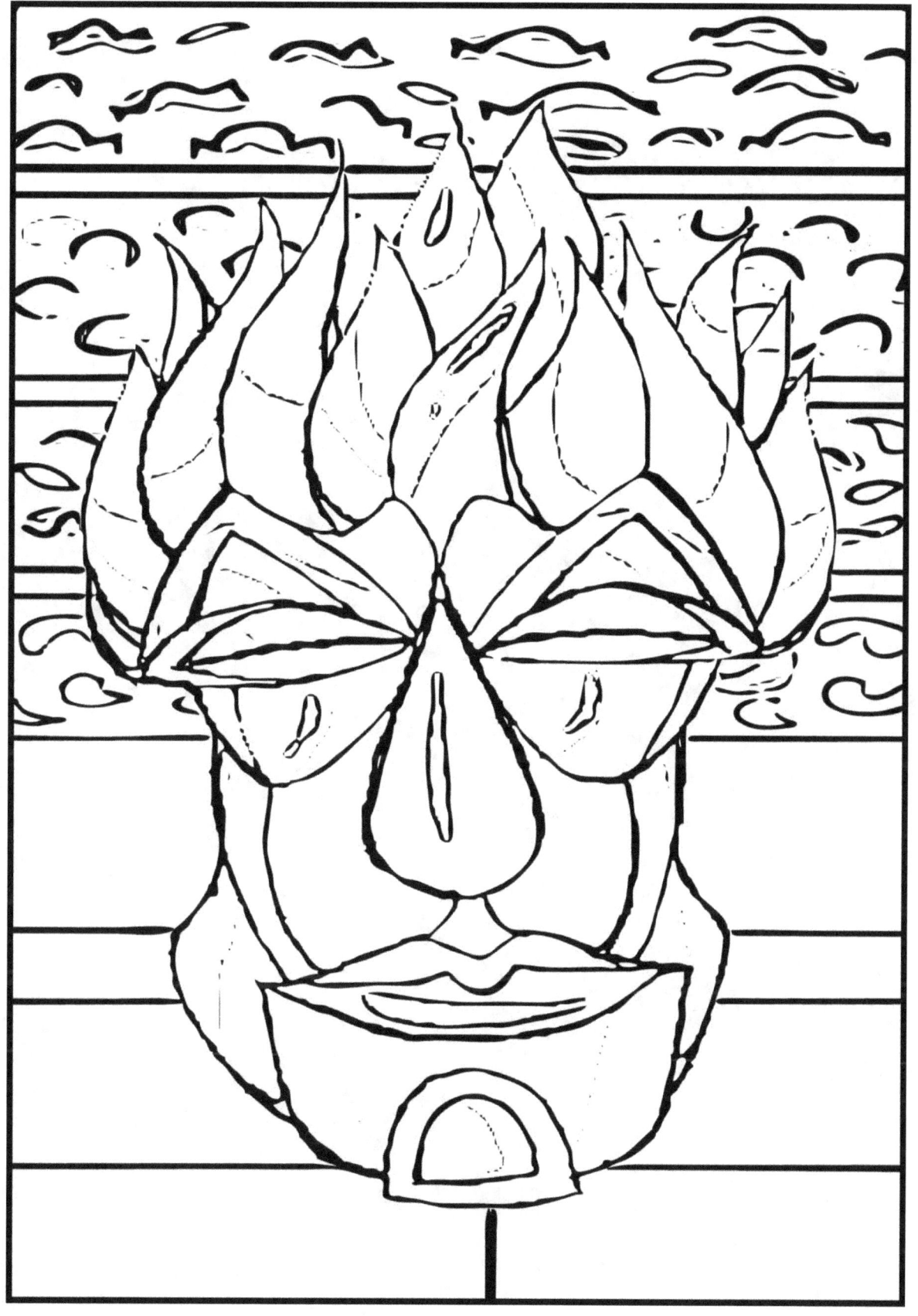

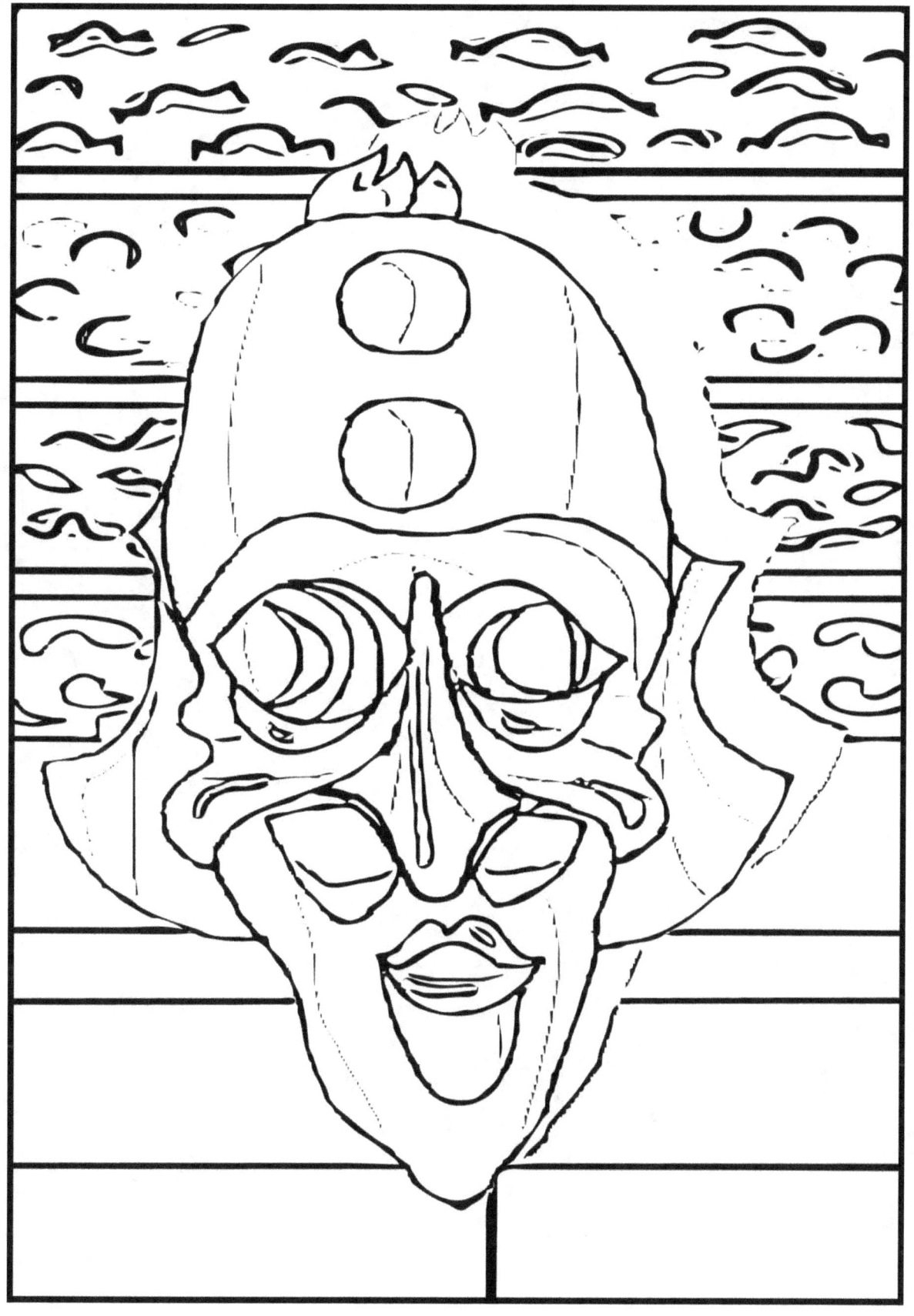

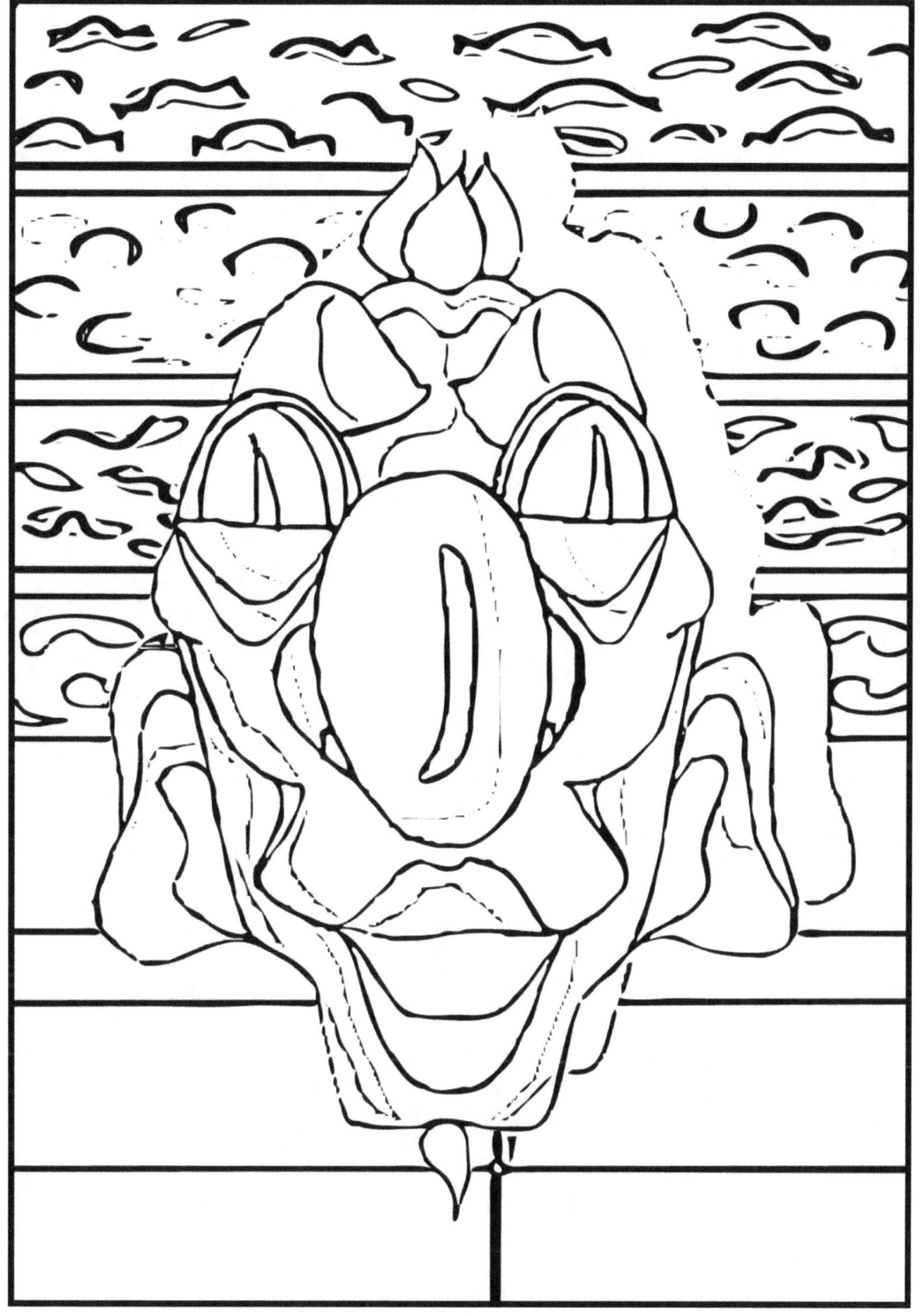

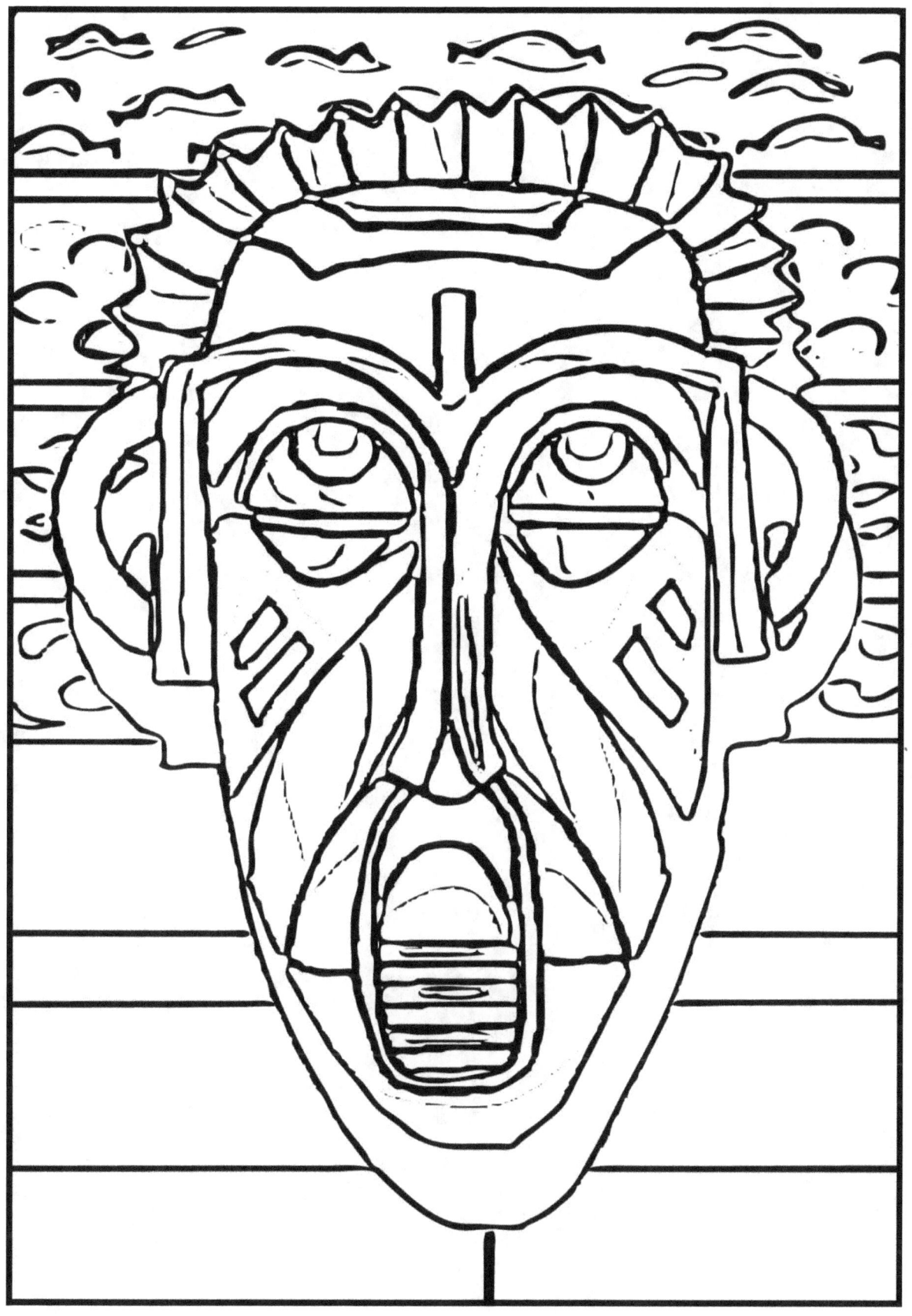

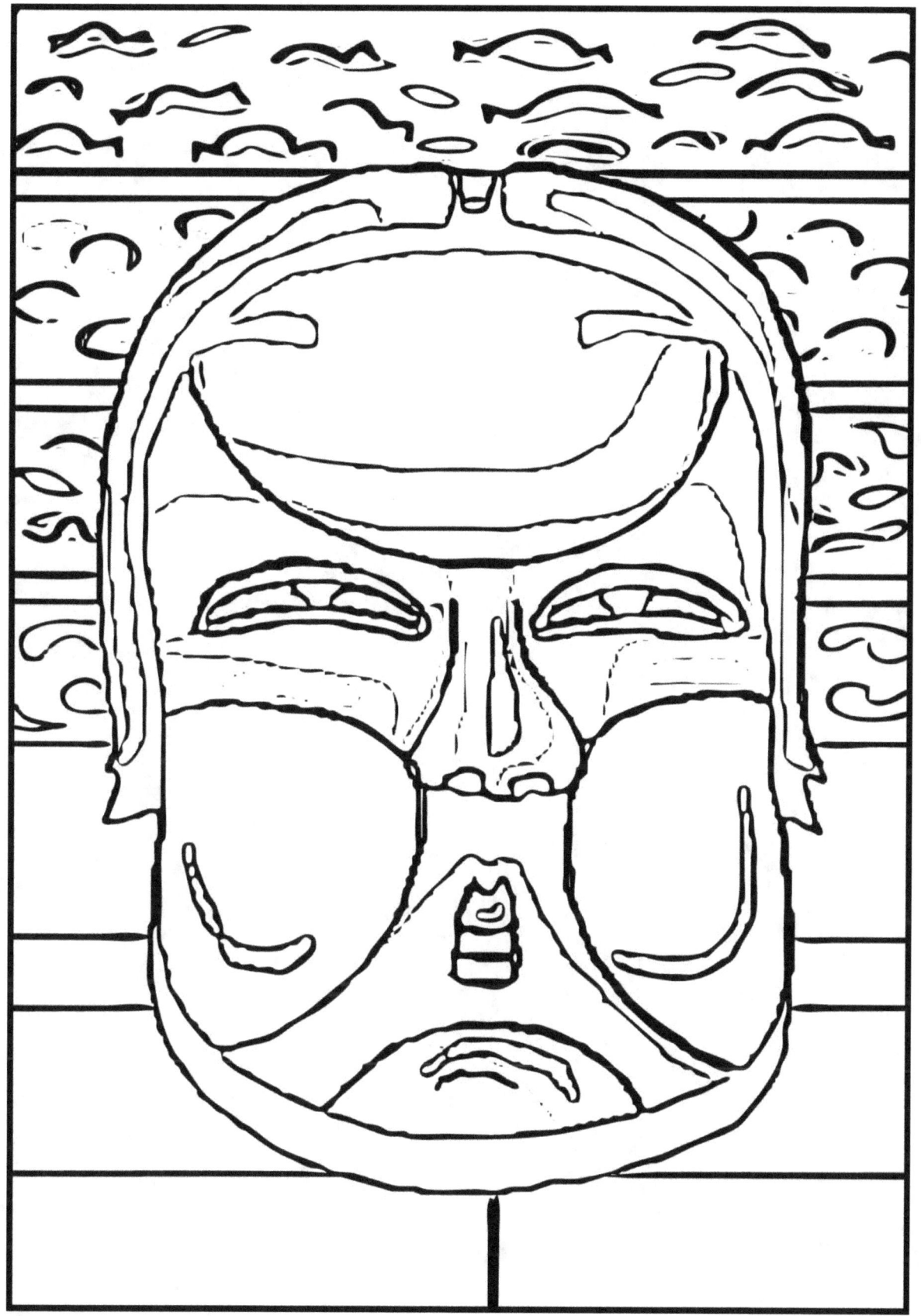

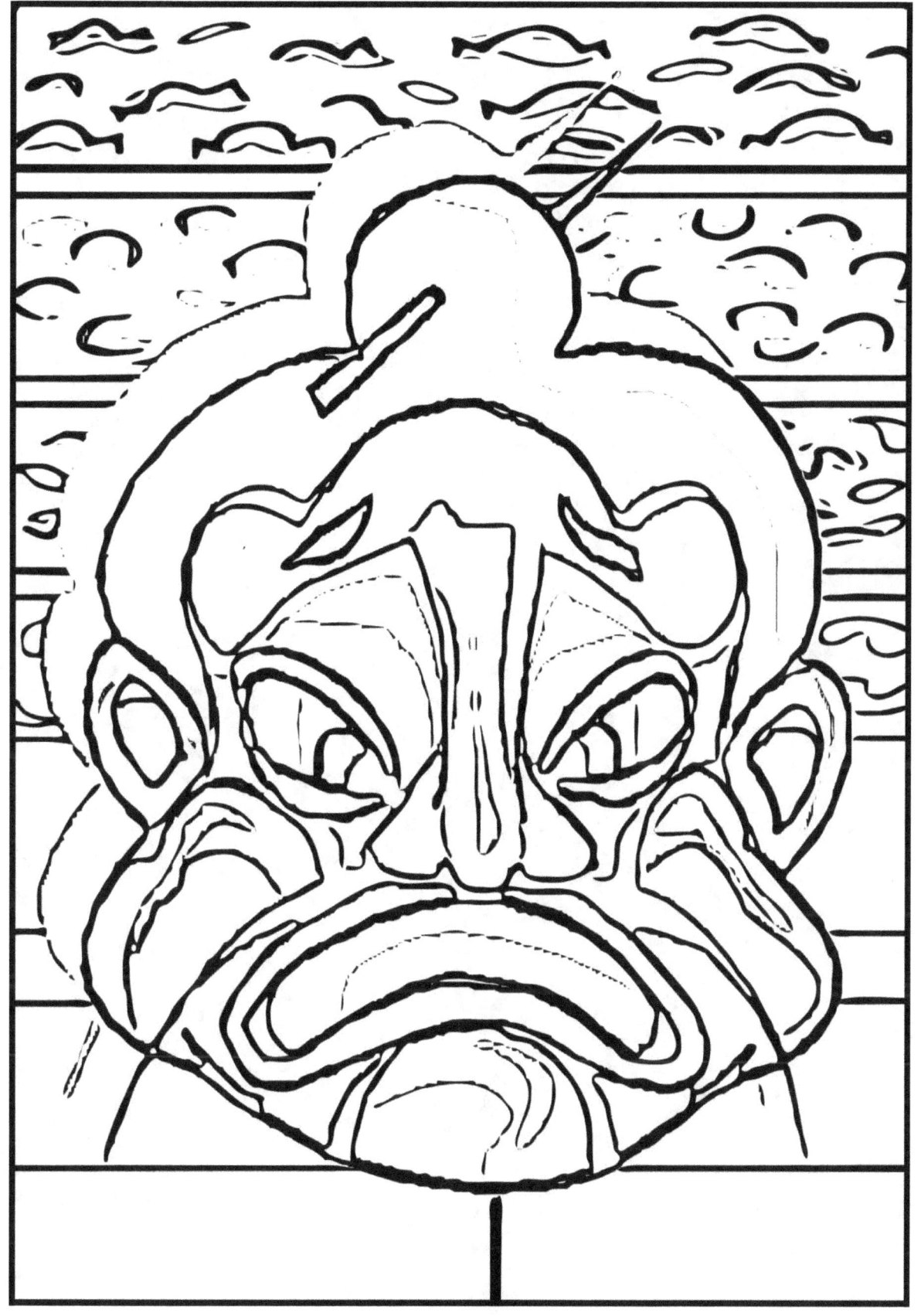

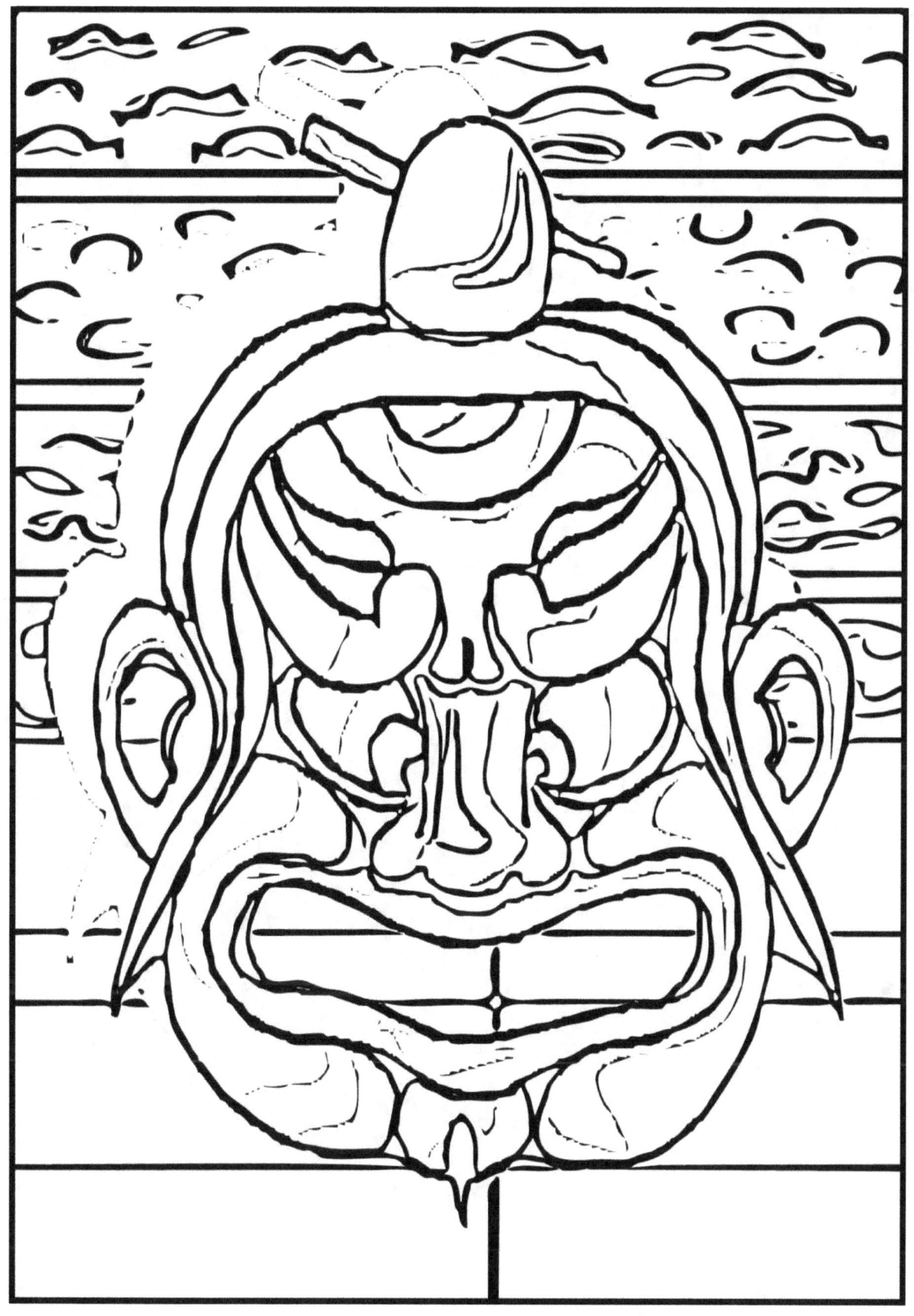

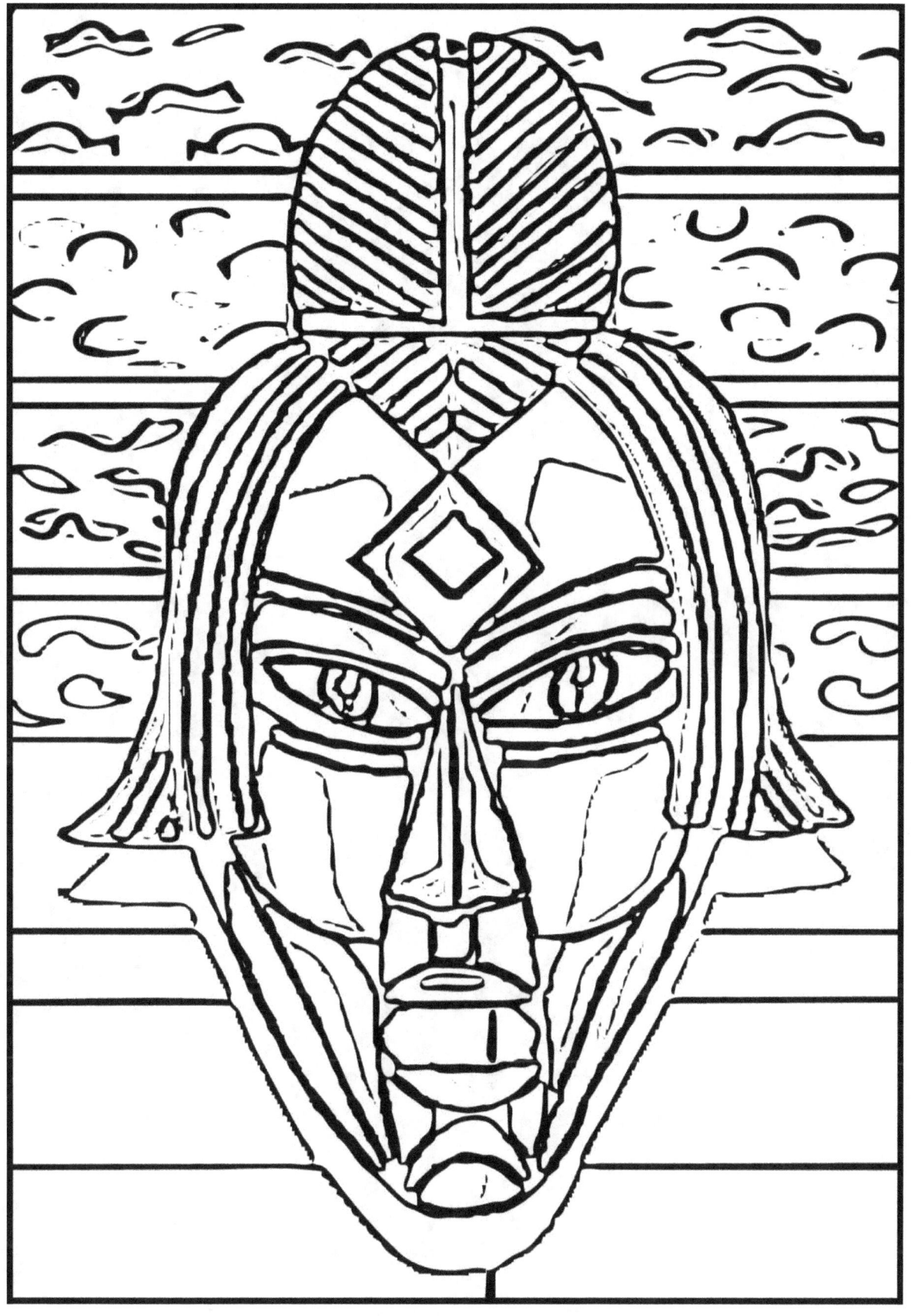

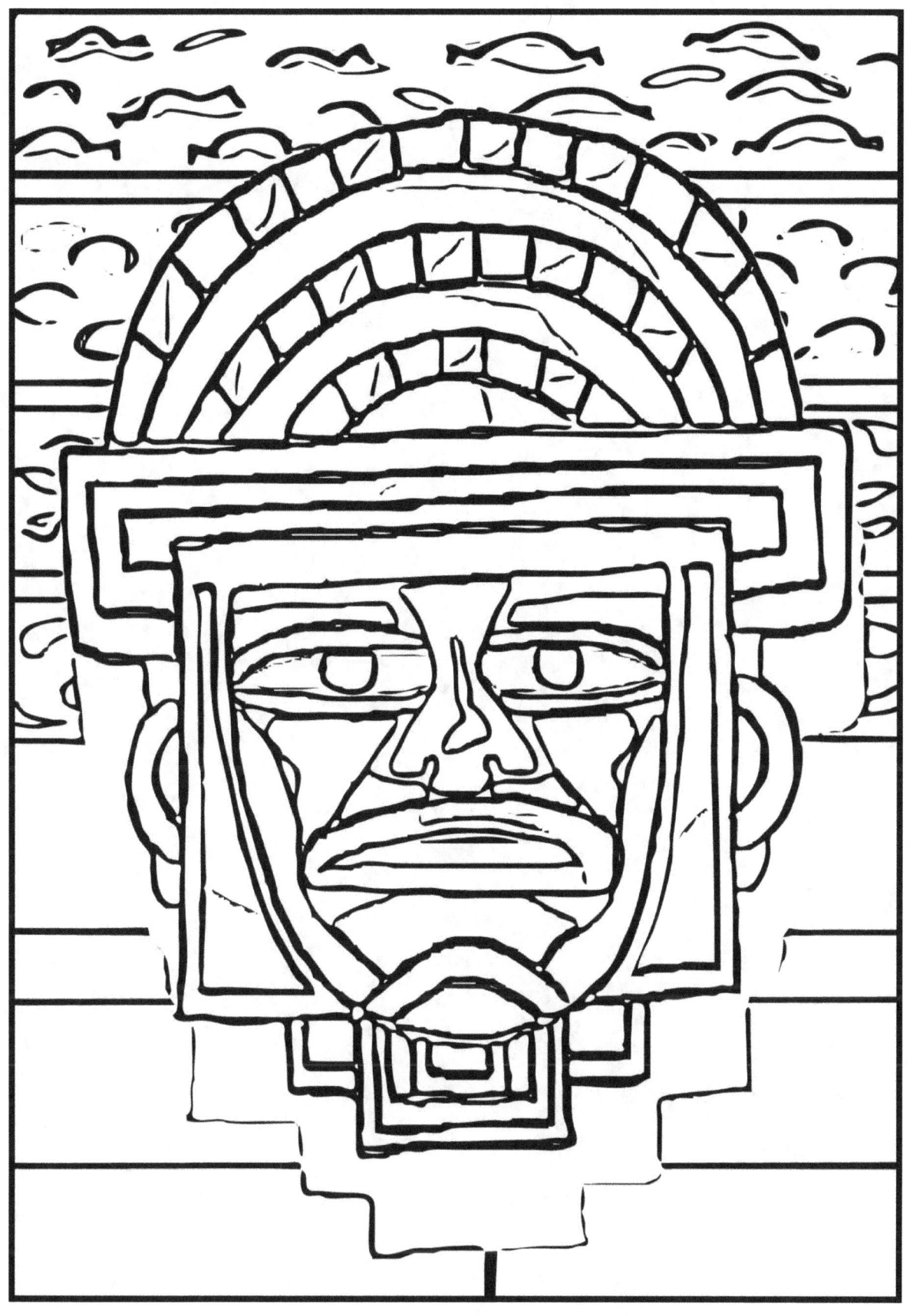

Beautiful Female Faces Coloring Book

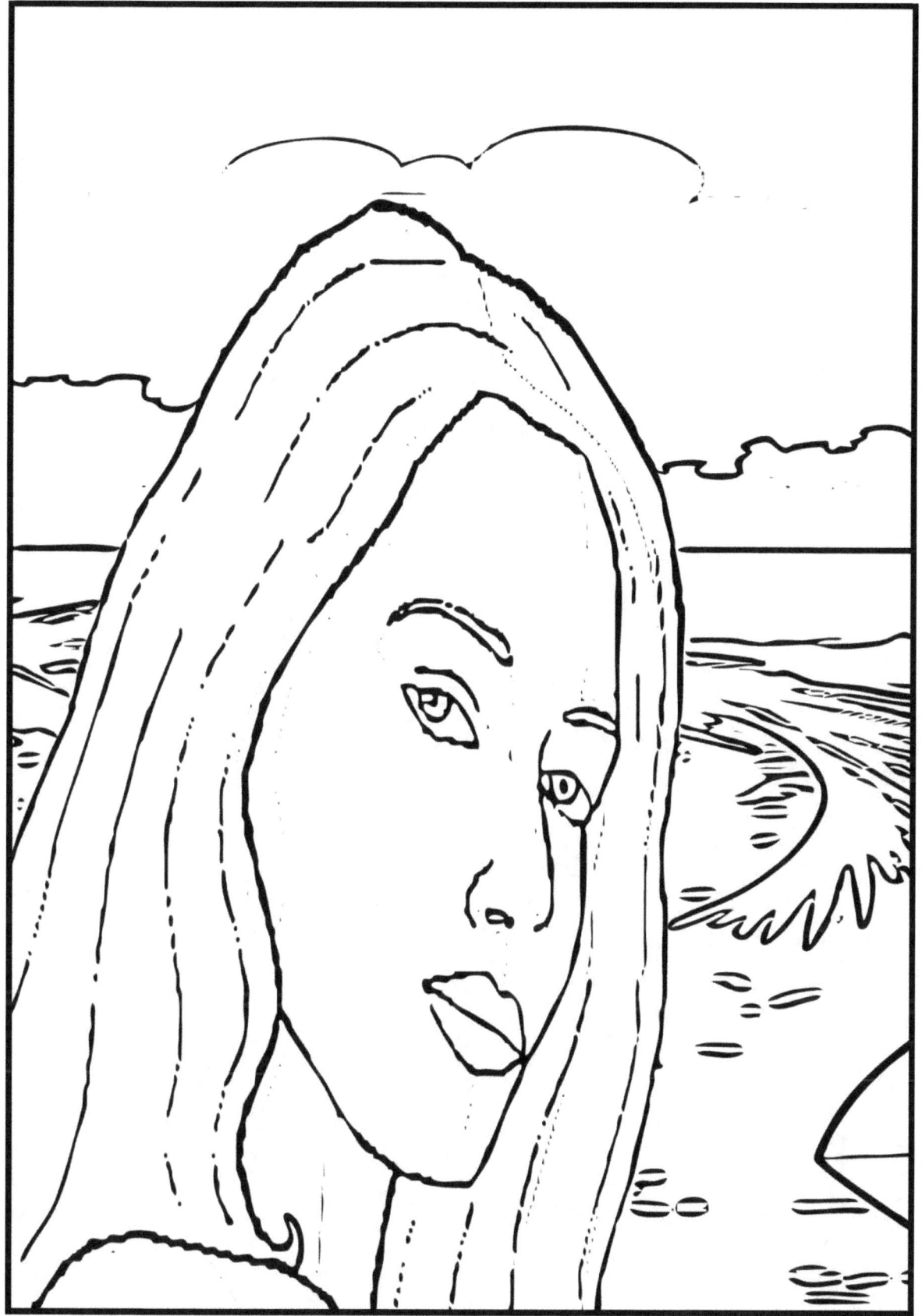

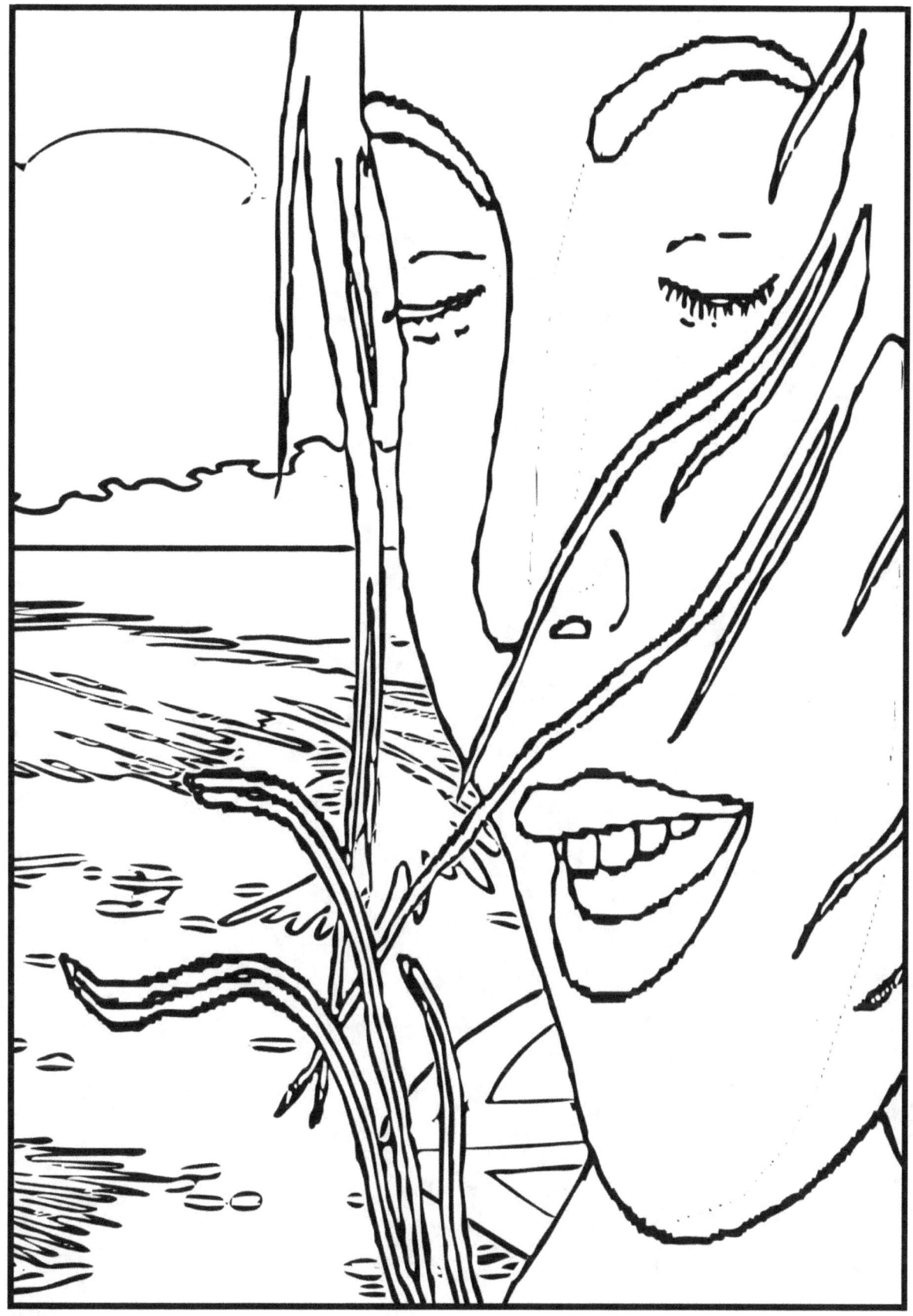

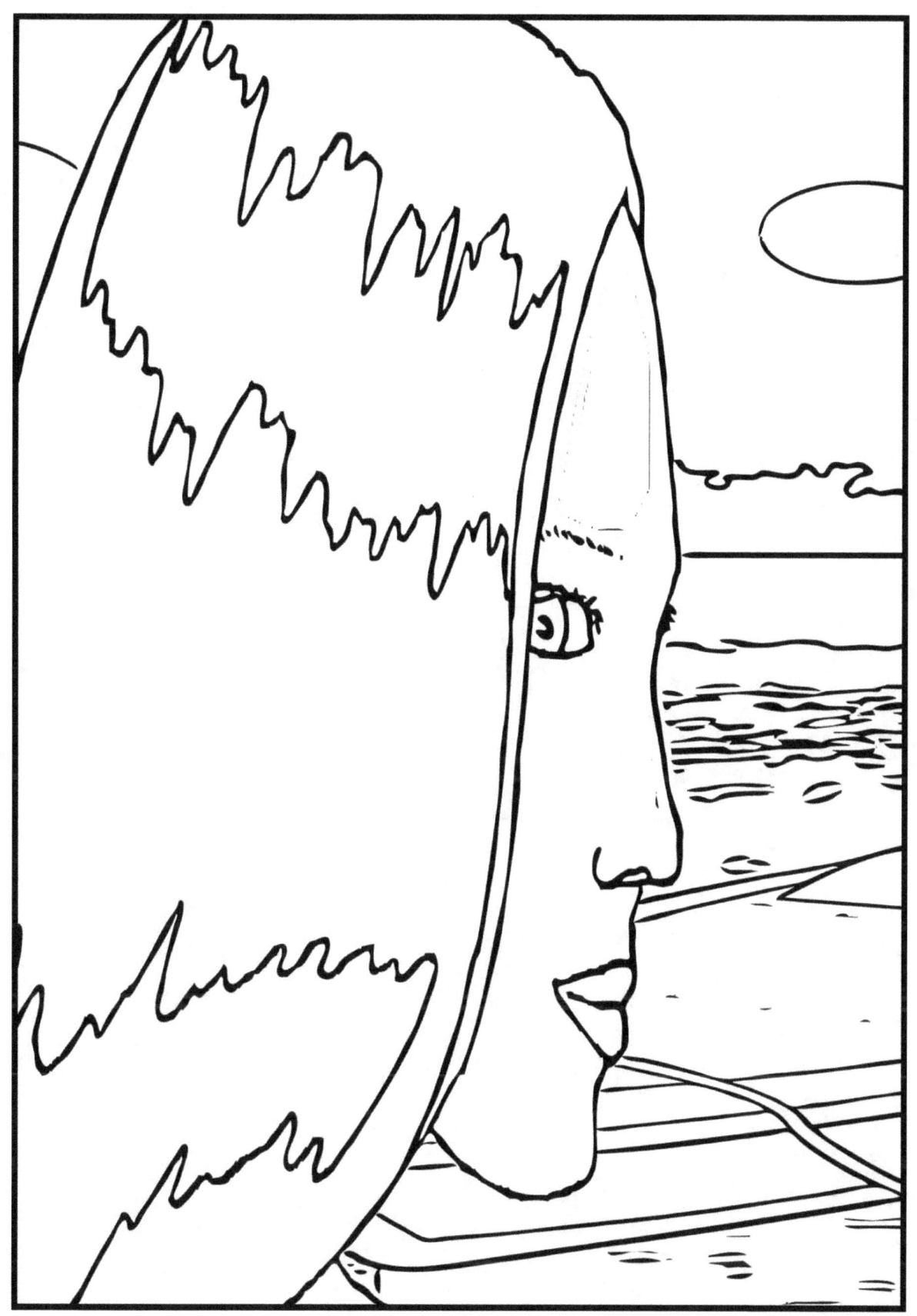

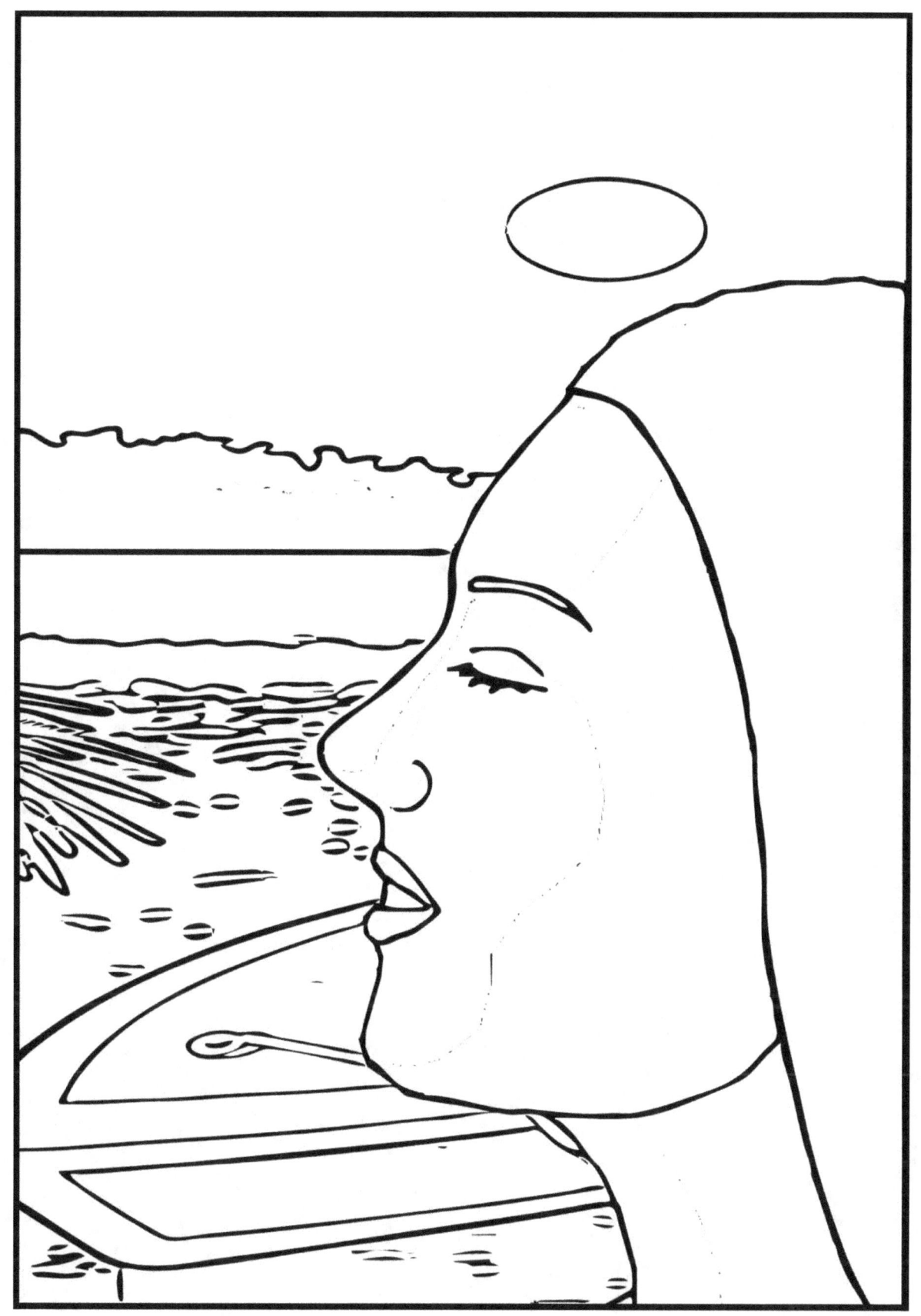

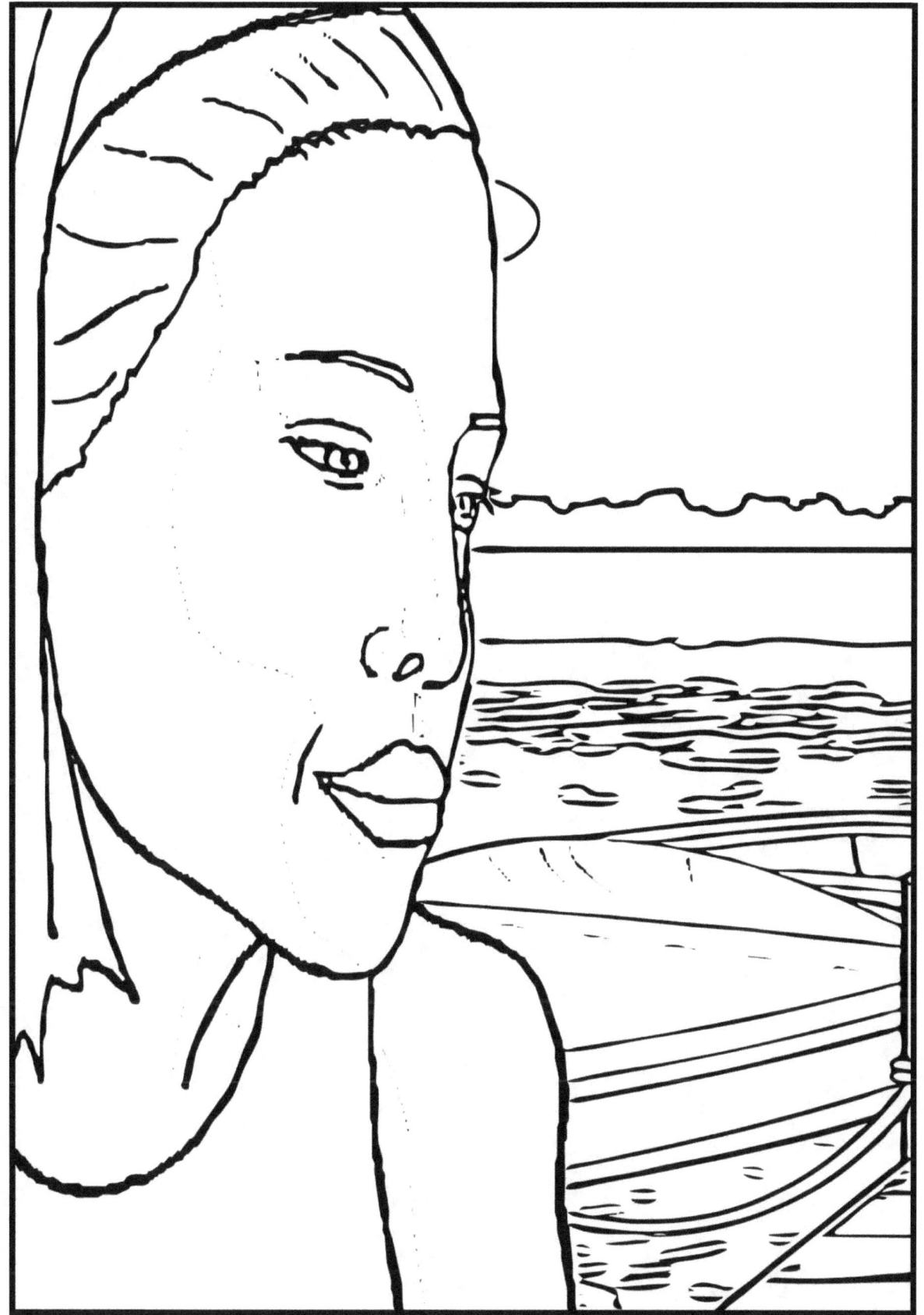

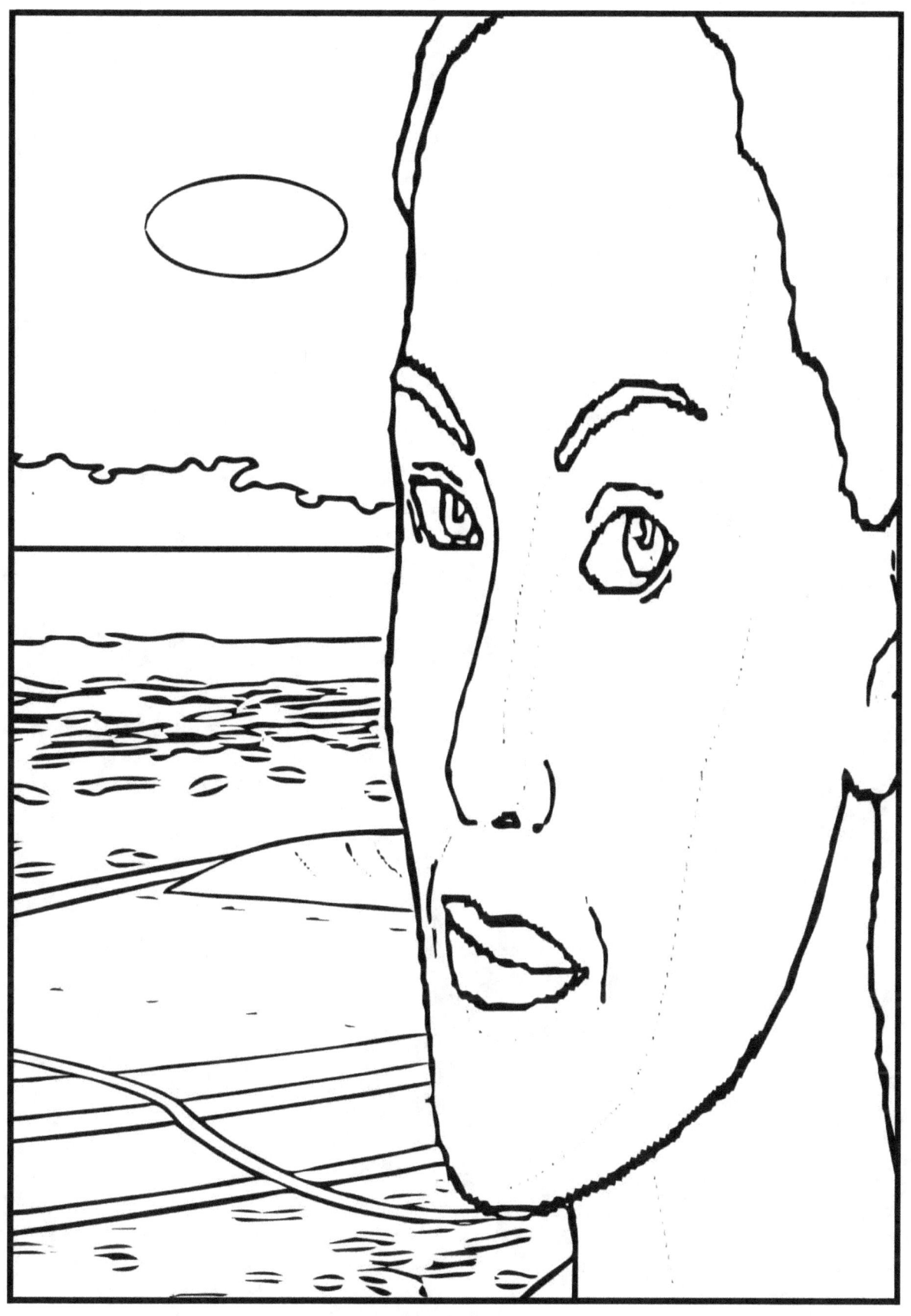

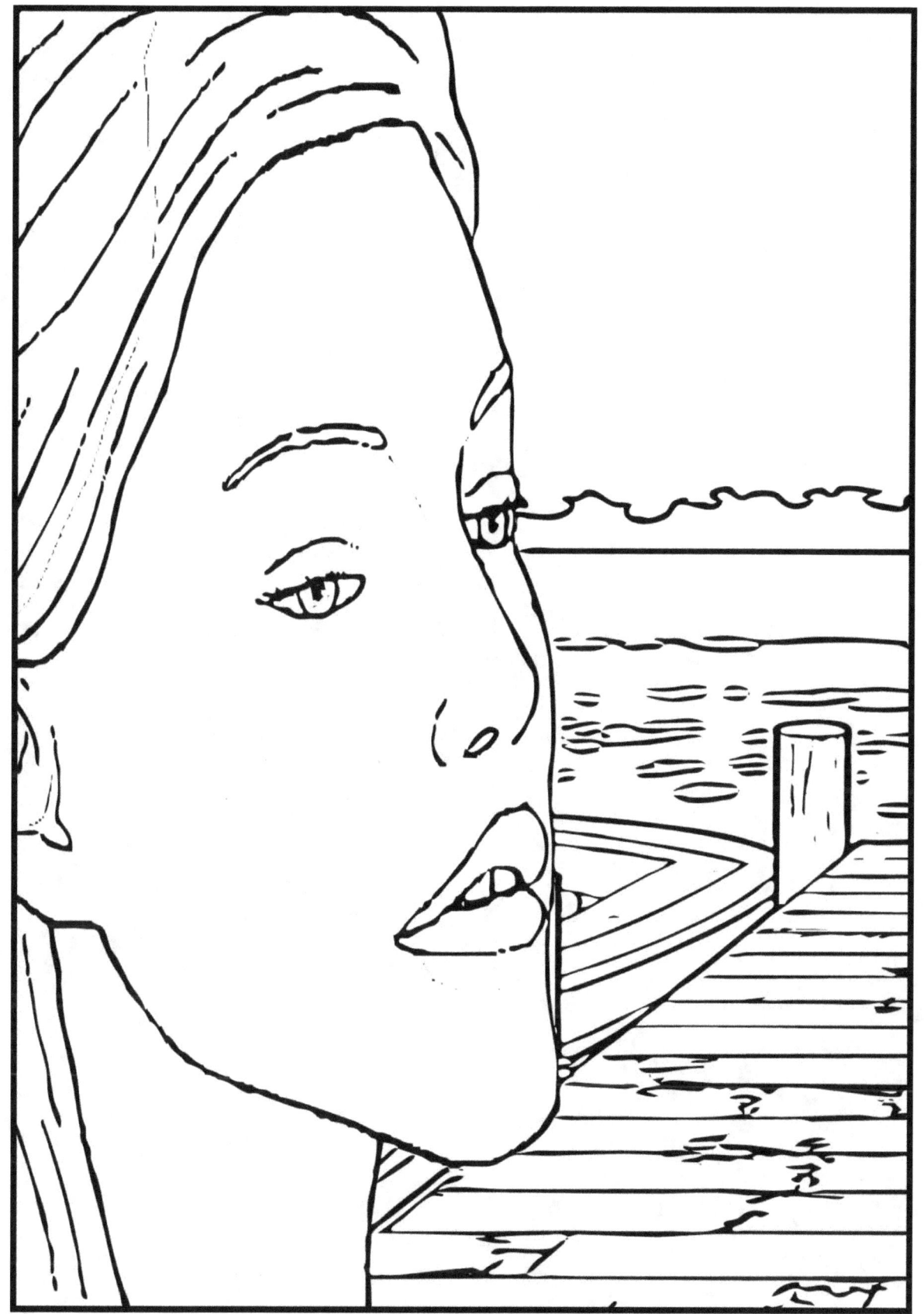

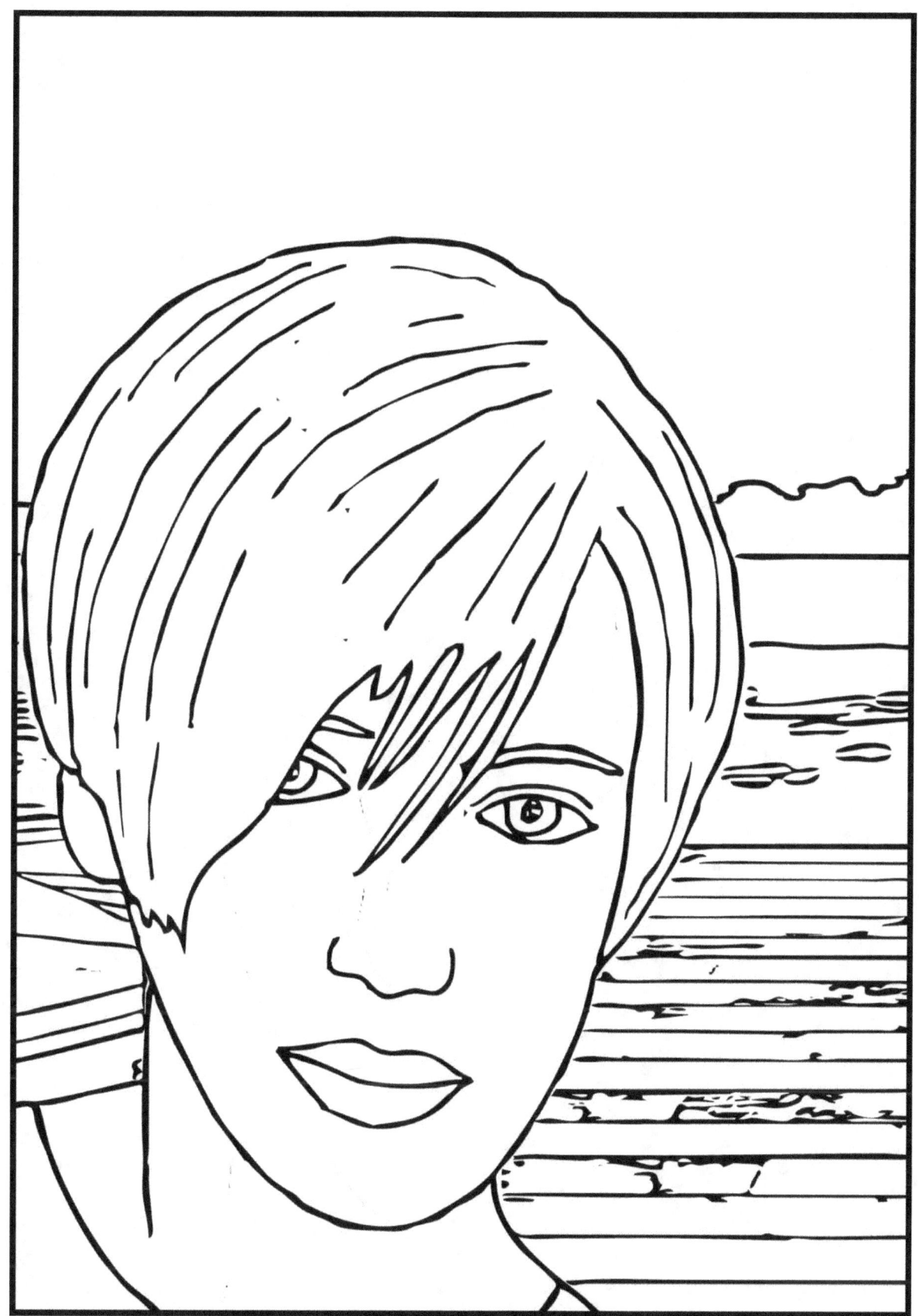

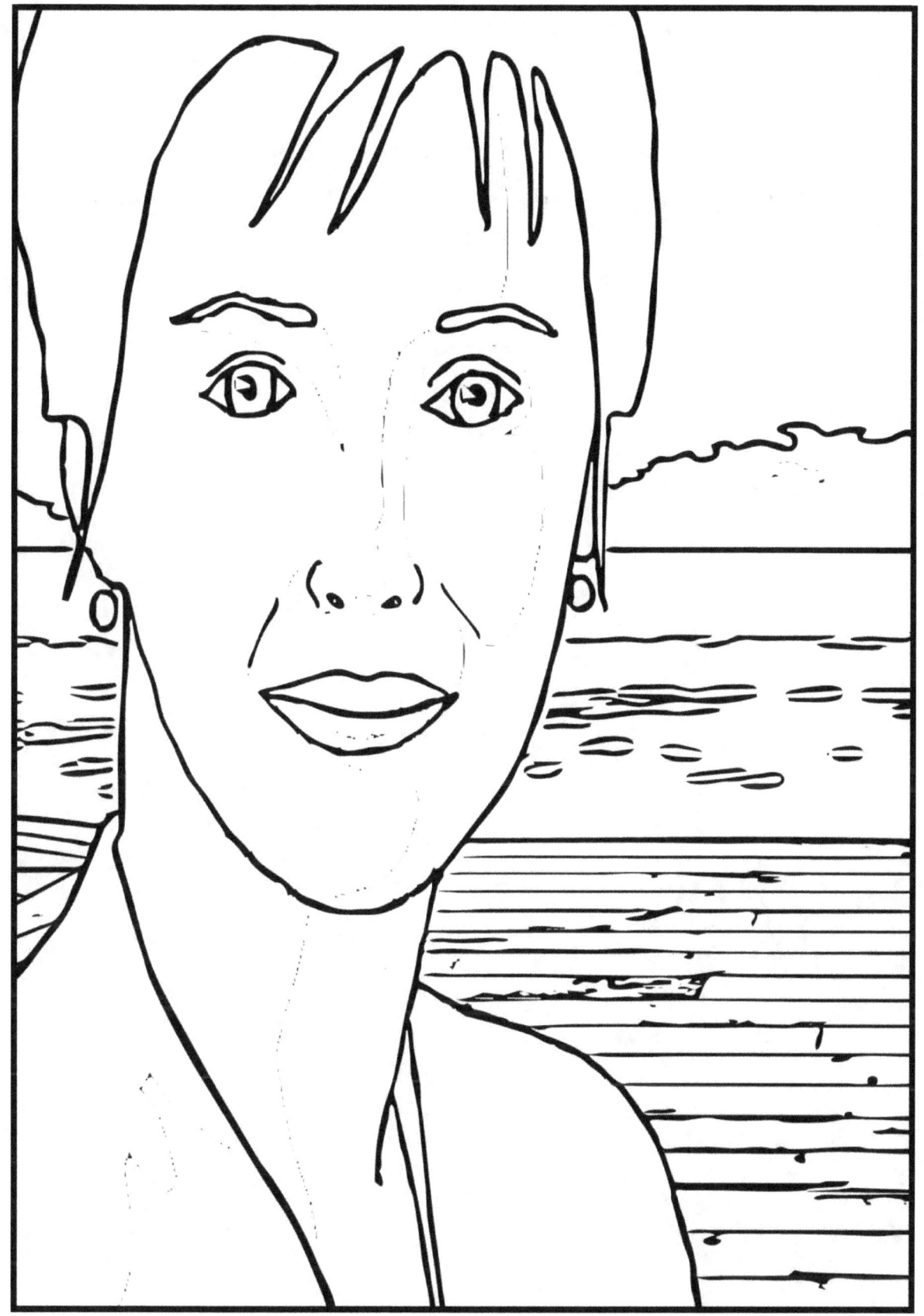

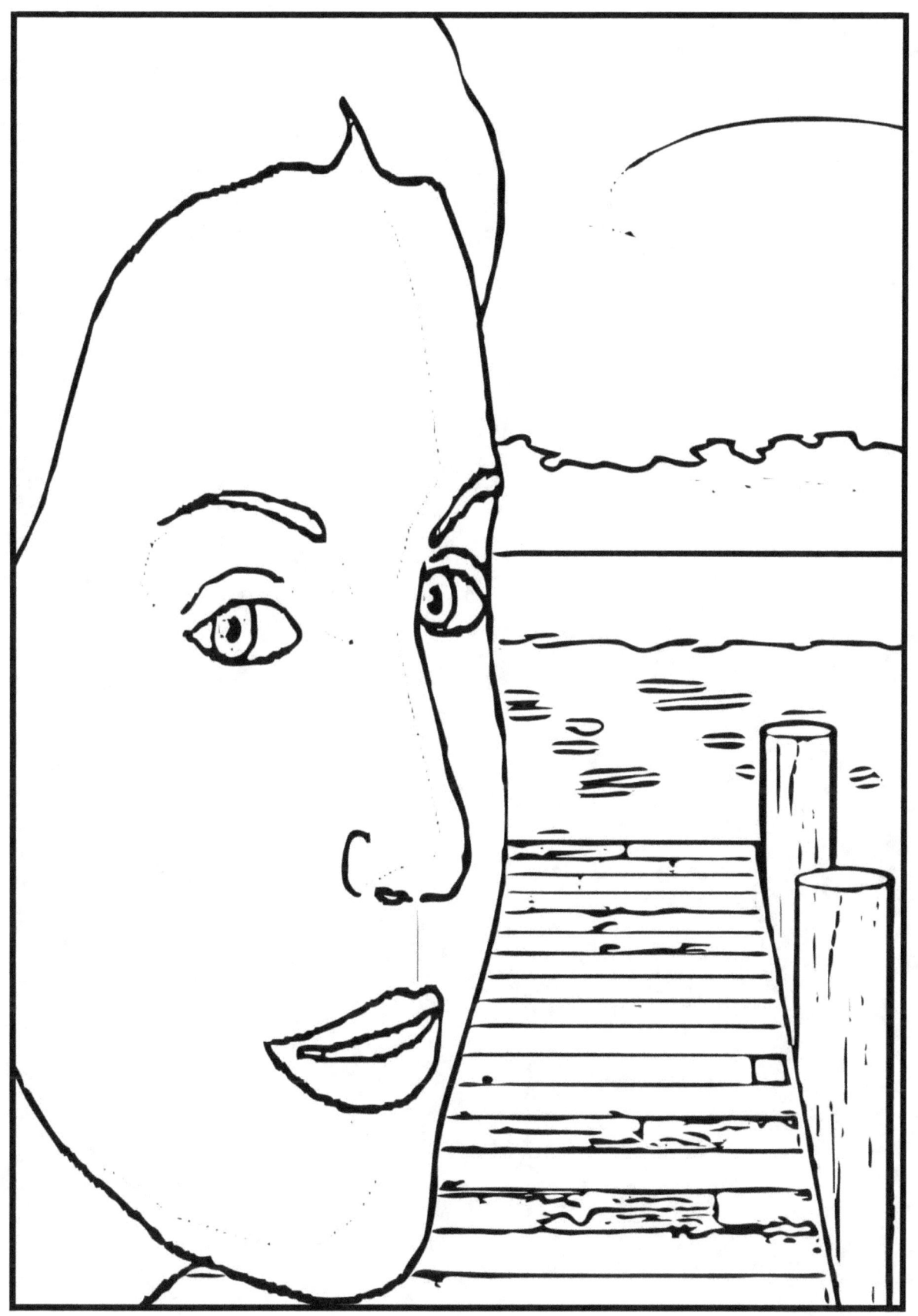

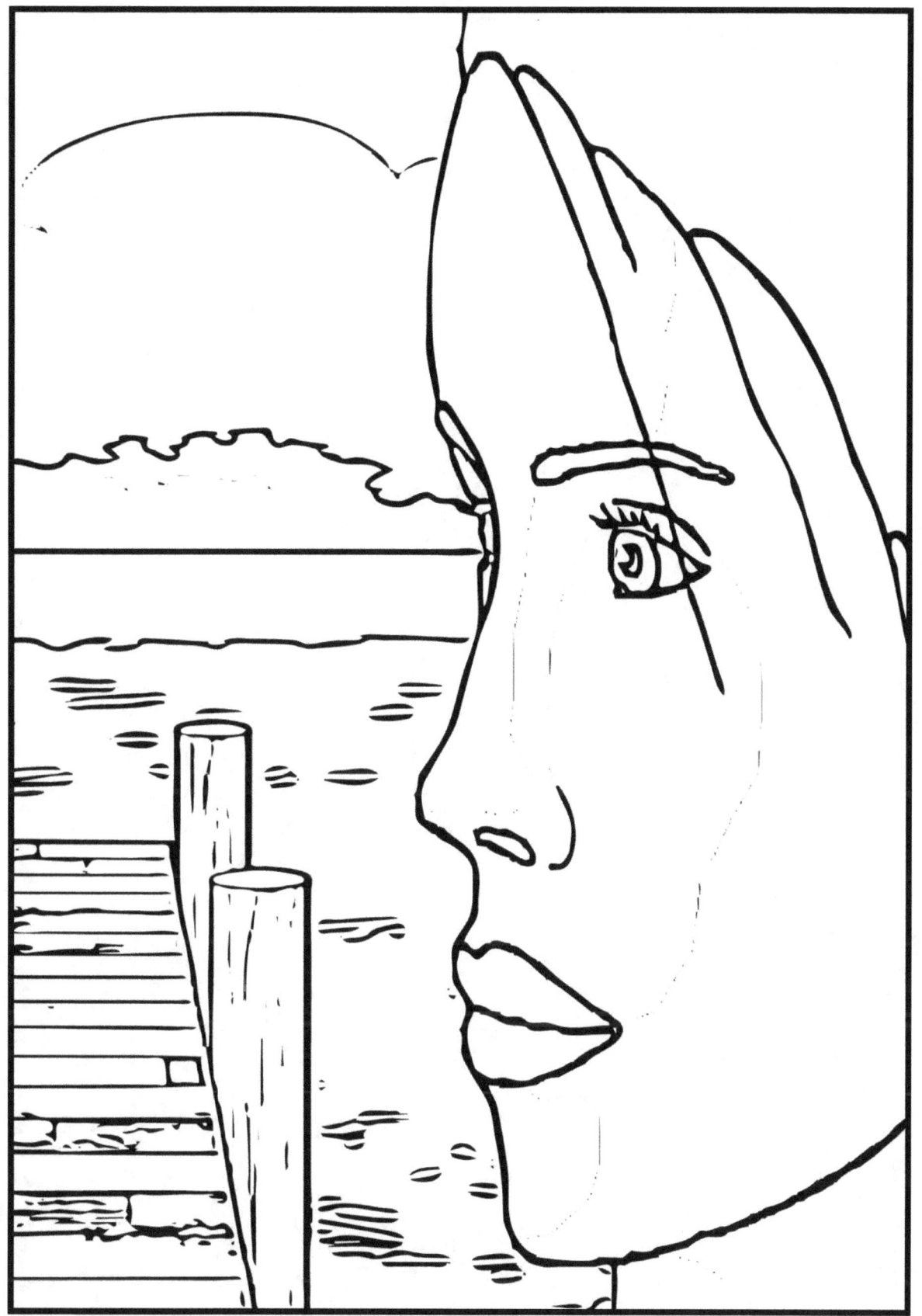

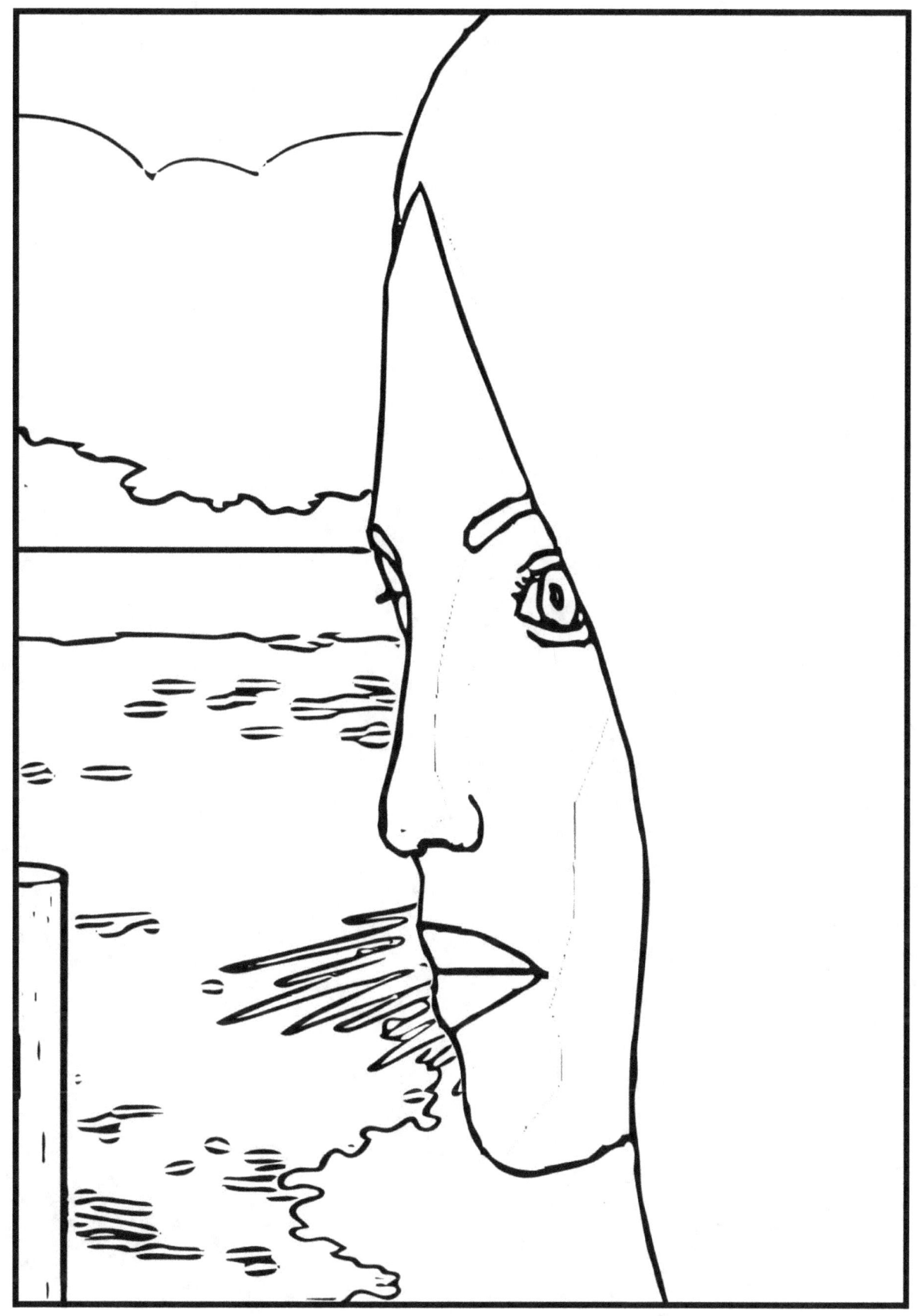

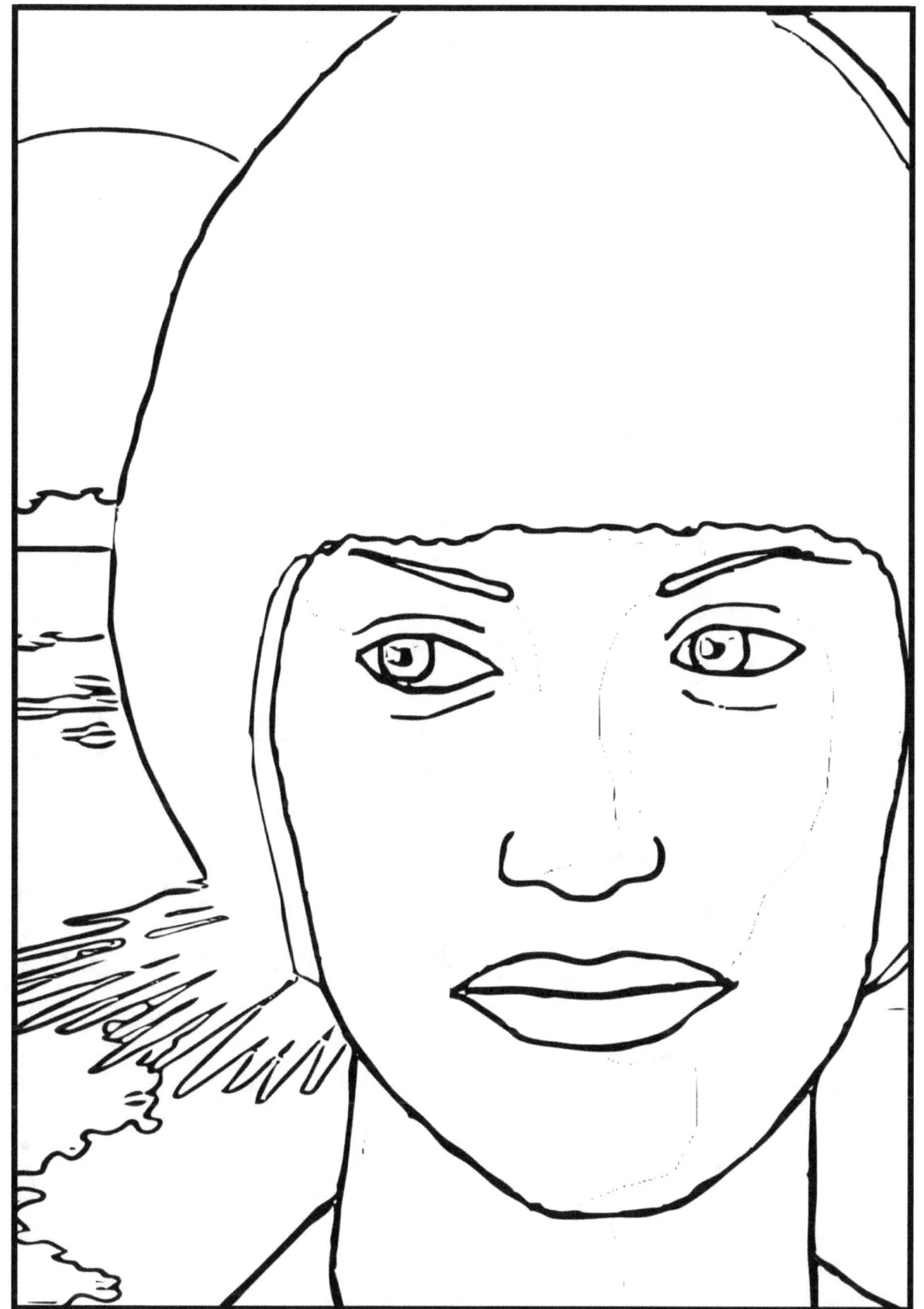

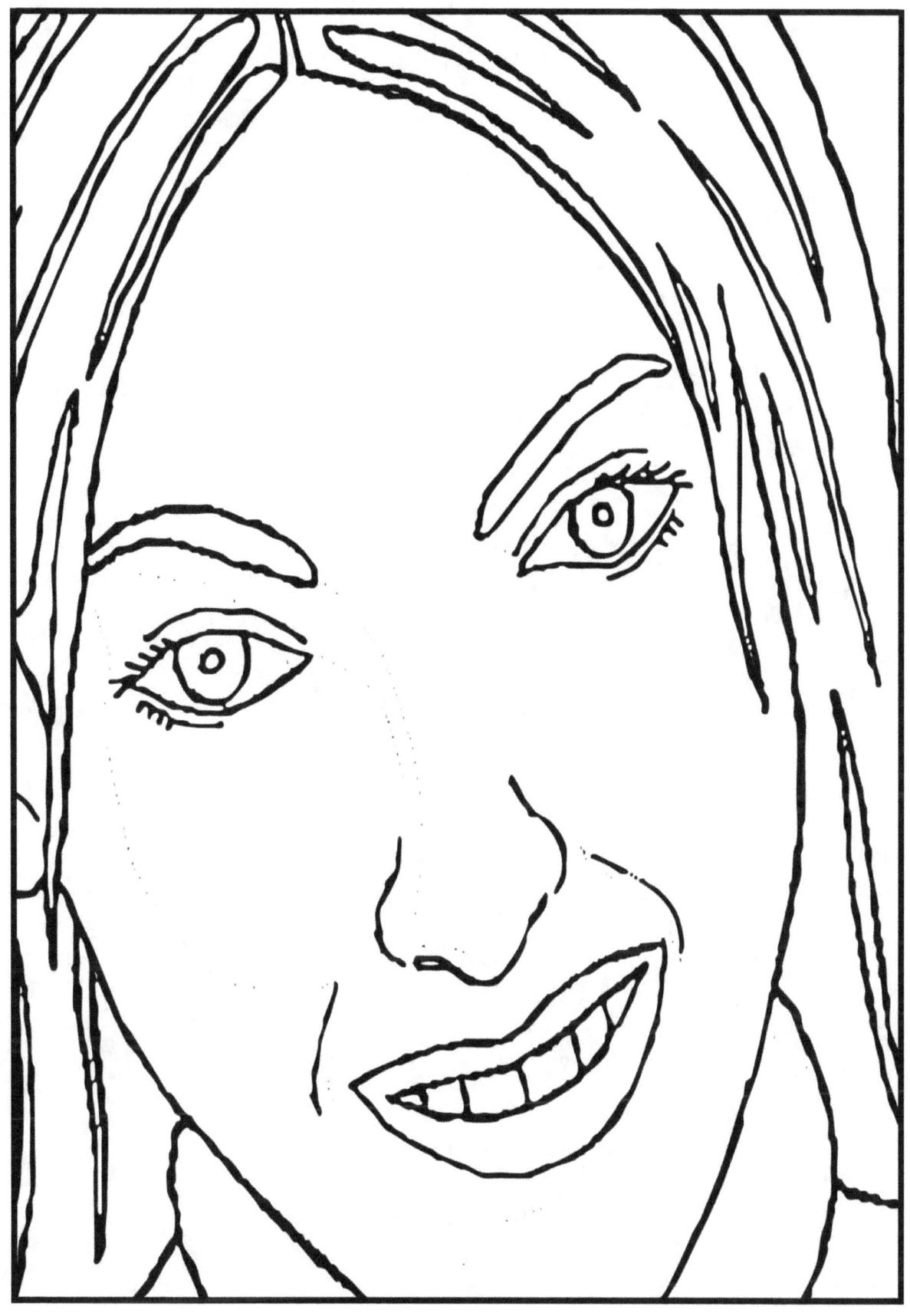

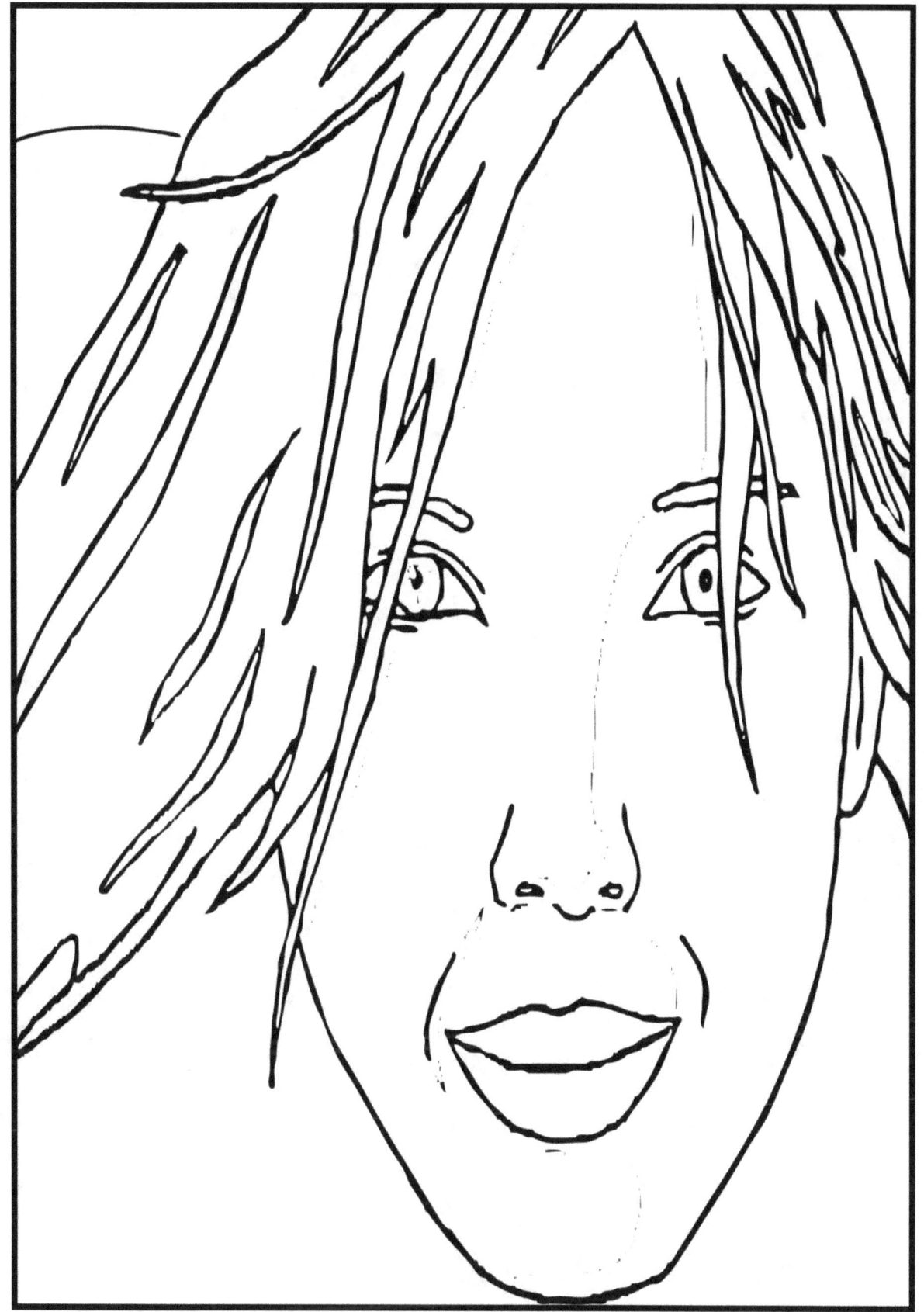

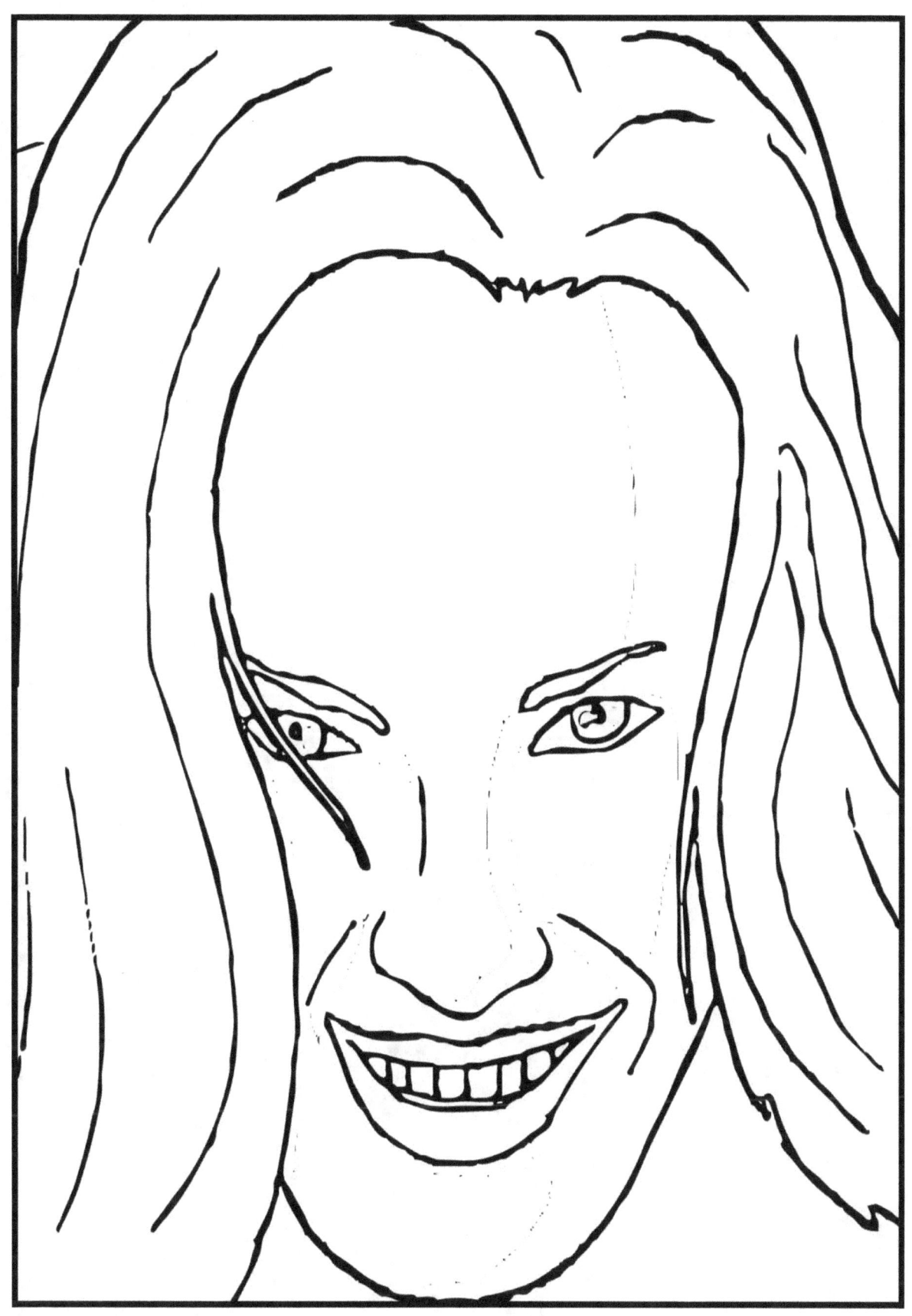

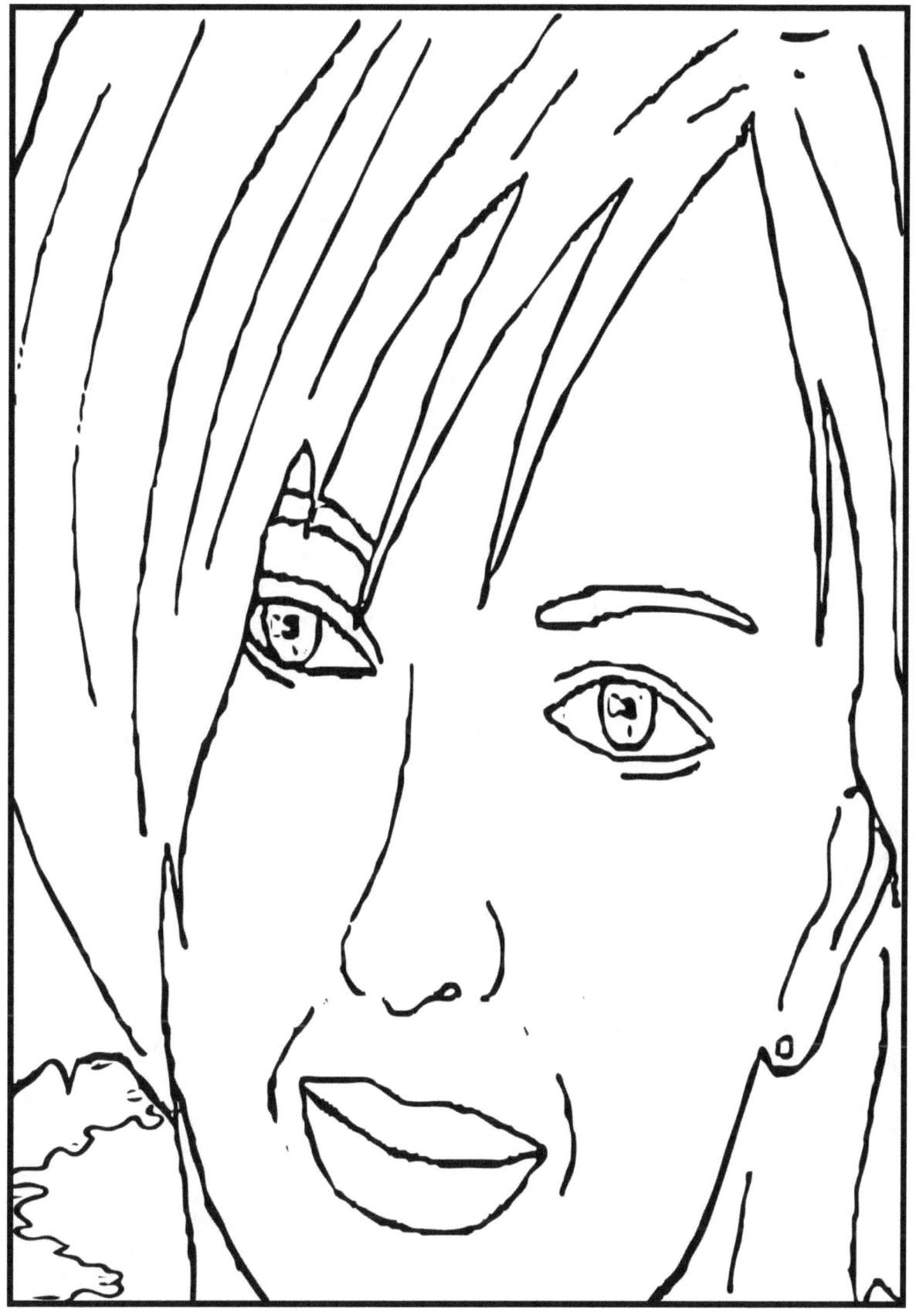

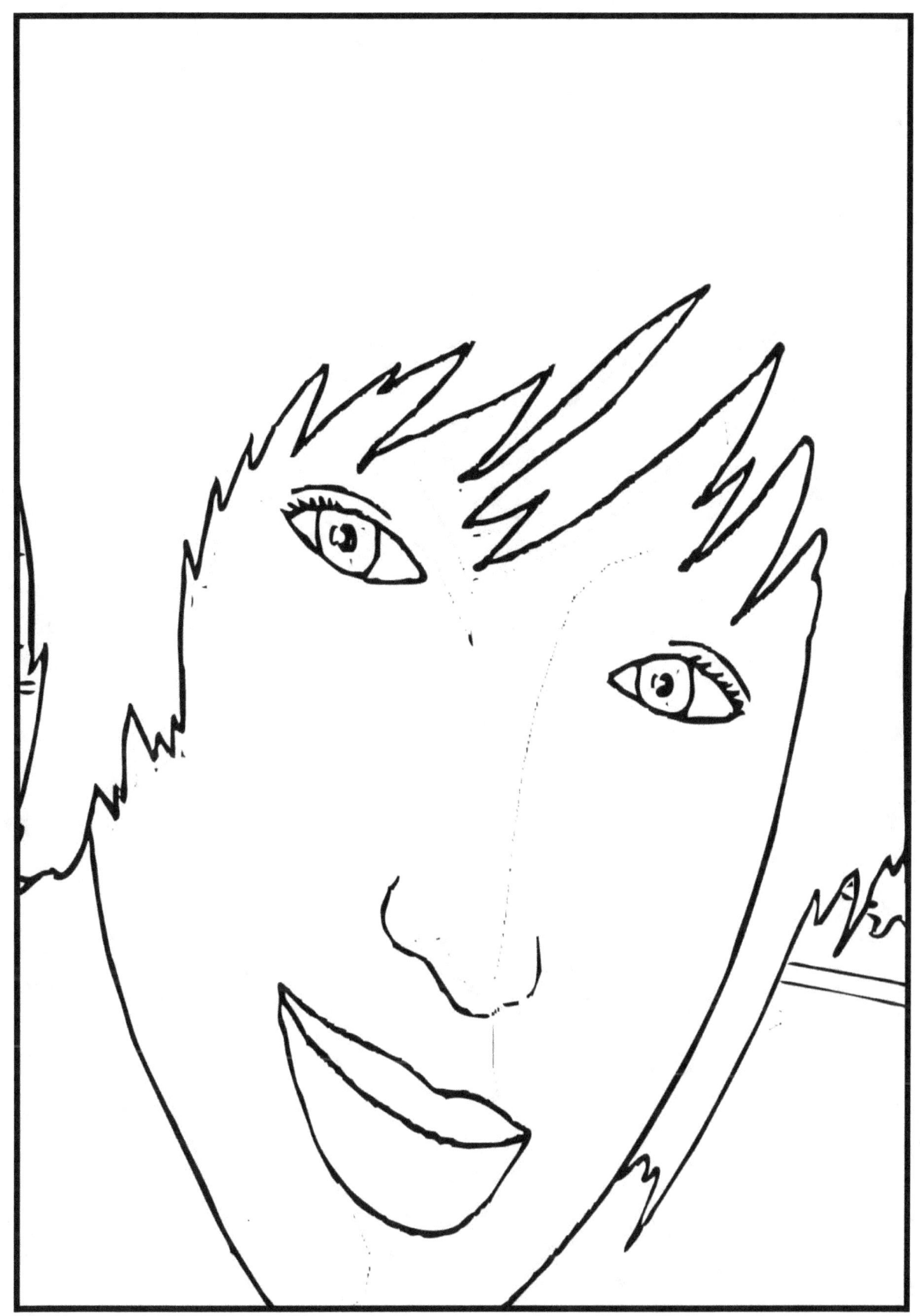

www.ingramcontent.com/pod-product-compliance
Lightning Source LLC
Chambersburg PA
CBHW081556170526
45166CB00009B/2716

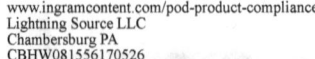